Baby with the Bath water

The expression "don't throw out the baby with the bath water" comes to mind when I think of the commonly held views of Pauline theology regarding the Law. Paul repeatedly emphasized the futility of utilizing or relying on the Law for salvation but that did not mean that Paul didn't love the Law and **consider himself a Law observing Jew *(Acts 21:24, Acts 24:14, Acts 25:8)*.** Christians often take the phrase "*not under the Law*" to mean that the Law is completely inoperative and without purpose in our lives. I believe that a careful examination of the scripture as a whole will promote the view that the Christian is not under the "*curse of the Law*", meaning its penalties, but that its righteous imperatives remain righteous just as they were during the 1600 years prior to the cross.

Gal 3:10-11
10 All who **rely on observing** the laws are under a curse, for it is written: "Cursed is everyone who does not continue to do everything written in the Book of the Law." 11 Clearly **no one is justified before God by the law**, because, "The righteous will live by faith."

Galatians makes the resounding point that relying on observing the Law for salvation brings about the penalties prescribed in the Law or the curse. This is because of man's inability to keep the Law. Jesus took this curse upon himself. He kept the Law perfectly and yet was punished in our place as a Law breaker. In this way He removed the penalty of the Law! Faithful trusting in his work and reliance upon his grace are the Christian's hope.

Gal 3:13
13 Christ redeemed us from the **curse of the law** by becoming a curse for us, for it is written: "Cursed is everyone who is hung on a tree."

As we move on to other areas of the scripture, I hope to be able to persuade you not to throw out the "baby" (**Law**) with the "bath water" (**curse of the Law**). In Christ there is no longer any condemnation caused by man's weakness and inability to keep the Law. Through Jesus' work in removing the penalty of the Law the believer is set free from the demand for our death as a result of sin (*law of sin and death*) and is empowered to keep the righteous requirements of the Law(*law of the Spirit of life*) in our new life in Christ.

Rom 8:1-4
8:1 Therefore, there is **now no condemnation** for those who are in Christ Jesus, 2 because through Christ Jesus the law of the Spirit of life set me free from the law of sin and death. 3 For what the law was powerless to do in that it was **weakened by the sinful nature**, God did by sending his own Son in the likeness of sinful man to be a sin offering. And so he condemned sin in sinful man, 4 in order that **the righteous requirements of the law might be fully met in us**, who do not live according to the sinful nature but according to the Spirit.

Law Don't Go Round Here, Law Dawg!

One of my favorite movies about the life and adventures of Wyatt Earp features a dramatic scene in which Ike Clanton takes his stand against Wyatt with the words, "**Law don't go round here, law dawg...**" Of course, Ike quickly changed his mind when confronted with the penalty for such a statement: A Colt Peacemaker pointed squarely between the eyes. Aside from the traditional themes of loyalty, vengeance, and macho bravado, the movie uses imperfect characters to emphasize that righteous standards are right even if the people implementing them are flawed.

Over the past twelve and a half years I have been blessed to be thoroughly enriched by sound biblical teaching. I am thankful and appreciative of the foundation that others worked to lay in my life. With all of my heart, I strive to build upon that foundation in order to advance the Kingdom and offer something of value to my brothers and sisters in Christ. As a pastor I have a responsibility and obligation to constantly evaluate the doctrine I teach to ensure that it is 'in line" with the teachings of the Apostles. In recent years the ministry of the Holy Spirit has led me to re-examine some of the views I have entertained regarding the Torah (five books of Moses). In practice I have always been a student of both the Older and Newer Testaments. The majority of the messages that I teach and preach on have been derived from the Tanakh (Older Testament). However, my view of the Mosaic revelation found in the Torah had always been somewhat paradoxical. While I taught about the "shadows and types" contained in the Torah as valid and meaningful to the average Christian, my general tone regarding the Law itself was negative. A misunderstanding of the Pauline epistles had given me the impression that the Law was something to be rejected as opposed to faith or at the very least something that stood in opposition to "being led by the Spirit". This view was more of an inward feeling than something I verbalized, but never the less, it was present. After a couple of trips to Israel and more exposure to both Judaism and Messianic Christianity some of my original premises are being reshaped. No doubt some will fear that any reverence or appreciation for the Law is a "Judaizing" influence but I am confident that this concern is unfounded. Judaizers were those who sought to impose the customs of Moses on Gentiles ***as a requirement for both salvation and acceptance.*** I am a Gentile, who has embraced Jesus by way of Faith alone! I have been baptized in God's Holy Spirit and walk in the power and freedom of a new life in Christ. My purpose in writing this is not to lay legalistic burdens upon believers but rather to bring the righteous intent of the Law into its proper focus. *(Note: because the Greek word "Nomos" rendered "Law or law" is used in the Newer Testament to refer to the Torah I use Law as a synonym for Torah)*

Let me go ahead and get my disclaimer out of the way:

****Faith is the only means of salvation!(**Eph 2:8**) No legalistic approach can bring about righteousness.(**Gal 3:10**) If we rely on any system for salvation we are damned because even the system (Law) given by God to his people through special revelation had a flaw...Men are weak and can't keep it.(**Rom 8:3**) Rather than justify, the Law points out the sin caused by our weakness.(**Rom 3:20**) This does not however make the Law sin(**Rom 7:7**). The Law is holy, spiritual, and just! (**Rom 7:12**)*

Clear Historical Record

The book of Acts is the history book of the early church. When faced with theological controversies arising from the scriptures, the book of Acts often provides us with the historical context or the *"practice of the Apostles"* displayed in their daily lives. A very common example that most of you will be familiar with is baptism. In **Matthew 28:19** Jesus gives instructions on baptism saying, *"…make disciples of all nations, baptizing them in the name of the Father and of the Son and of the Holy Spirit."* We then see that the book of Acts records the Apostles baptizing in *the name of Jesus **(Acts 2:38, Acts 10:48, Acts 19:5).*** In the face of an apparent contradiction, most Christians have relied on the book of Acts to give insight into how the early church understood the words of Jesus. Without going into the entire argument, the summation is that **the book of Acts clearly displays what the Apostles understood Matthew 28:19 to mean!** This practice of utilizing the book of Acts to provide historical context for difficult passages of scripture is well accepted within most evangelical circles. I think, then, that it is fitting to see how the book of Acts portrays Paul and the other believer's view of the Law.

Acts 21:20-24
20 When they heard this, they praised God. Then they said to Paul: "You see, brother, how many thousands of **Jews have believed, and all of them are zealous for the law**. 21 They have been informed that you teach all the Jews who live among the Gentiles to turn away from Moses, telling them not to circumcise their children or live according to **our** customs. 22 What shall we do? They will certainly hear that you have come, 23 so do what we tell you. There are four **men with us** who have made a vow. 24 Take these men, join in

their purification rites and pay their expenses, so that they can have their heads shaved. **Then everybody will know there <u>is no truth in these</u> reports about you, but that <u>you</u> yourself <u>are living in obedience to the law</u>.**

An unbiased reading of the plain text supports the concept that the early community of believers was *"zealous for the Law"* and that Paul was living in what James and the Elders considered *"obedience to the Law"*. In fact, Paul goes on to comply with the suggestions of James and the Elders for the stated purpose of displaying that there *"was/is no truth in these reports about you…"* What were the reports? What was the rumor that the righteous men sought to squelch? The answer is in the text, *"They have been informed that you* **'Paul'** *teach all the Jews who live among the Gentiles to turn away from Moses, telling them not to circumcise their children or live according **to our customs**."* Why did Paul go along with the suggestion and take a Nazarite vow? Why were James and the Elders concerned about this *"report"* if it was in fact true? <u>The unavoidable conclusion is that the report was false and that Paul complied with the request to show the absurdity of the claim.</u> At the very least this information should be considered when examining Paul's letters. I found it interesting that *2 Peter* may contain commentary on this kind of misinformation regarding Paul:

2 Peter 3:15-18
15 Bear in mind that our Lord's patience means salvation, just as our dear brother **Paul** also wrote you with the wisdom that God gave him. 16 He writes the same way in all his letters, speaking in them of these matters. <u>His letters contain some things that are hard to understand, which ignorant and unstable people distort, as they do the other Scriptures</u>, to their own destruction.

17 Therefore, dear friends, since you already know this, be on your guard so that you **may not be carried away by the error of lawless men** and fall from your secure position.

What could Peter be talking about? Is it possible that Peter was aware that false reports were being circulated about Paul? Since Paul himself, while discussing the Law, says in ***Rom 3:8*** that he was being slandered---could it be that *Acts 21, 2 Peter3*, and ***Romans 3*** all have in view a misunderstanding of Paul's views on the Law? Look again at *2 Peter 3:17 "Therefore, dear friends, since you already know this, be on your guard so that you may not be carried away by the **error of (Athesmon)lawless men** and fall from your secure position."* The Complete Word Study Dictionary defines the Greek word "*Athesmon*" as without Law or accepted customs. The NIV rightly renders this "lawless"! Isn't that essentially what the rumor was in *Acts 21*? Apparently, Paul's letters and ministry have always generated controversy regarding our relationship to the Law. Remember...In *Acts 21* Paul took deliberate steps to prove that he was *"living in obedience to the law"* in an effort to silence lies about his teaching.

Please notice in *Acts 21* that the discussion had nothing to do with Gentile believers and their relationship to the Law that issue had already been addressed in *Acts 15* by these same men (Peter, Paul, and James). Instead the topic of discussion was the Jewish believers and their relationship to the Law. I will come back to that issue later on; but for now, let's go on to examine the historical context or "practice of the Apostles" as recorded in the book of Acts.

Acts 22:12-16
12 "A man named Ananias came to see me. He **was a devout observer of the law** and highly respected by all the Jews living there. 13 He stood beside me and said, 'Brother Saul, receive your sight!' And at that very moment I was able to see him.

14 "Then he said: 'The God of our fathers has chosen you to know his will and to see the Righteous One and to hear words from his mouth. 15 You will be his witness to all men of what you have seen and heard. 16 And now what are you waiting for? Get up, be baptized and wash your sins away, calling on his name.'

This is the same Ananias from *Acts 9*. Paul is recounting his testimony and he described Ananias as *"a devout observer of the Law"*. The very person that had an extended conversation with Jesus in *Acts 9* and who baptized Paul, healed Paul, and affirmed Paul's commission as an Apostle is being described as a devout observer of the Law. Please beware of thinking that the word *"was"* being in past tense means that Ananias used to be a devout observer of the Law and is no longer! The word is in the past tense because at the time of Paul's conversion Ananias (who was having extended conversations with Jesus) **was a devout observer of the Law**. In other words, the guy Jesus picked to go and speak to Paul at the time of Paul's conversion was obviously a believer in Yeshua (Jesus) and was a devout observer of the Law! Are these isolated incidents within the book of Acts or are there other clues as to the view that Paul had of the Law?

Acts 24:14-18
14 However, I admit that I worship the God of our fathers as a follower of the Way, which they call a sect. **I believe everything that agrees with the**

Law and that is written in the Prophets, 15 and I have the same hope in God as these men, that there will be a resurrection of both the righteous and the wicked. 16 So I strive always to keep my conscience clear before God and man.

17 "After an absence of several years, I came to Jerusalem to bring my people gifts for the poor and to present offerings. 18 **I was ceremonially clean** when they found me in the temple courts doing this.

Surely Paul's own words can be considered when shaping our view of his doctrine. Paul said that he "*agrees with the Law*" and he referred to himself as "*ceremonially clean*". This testimony from the book of Acts should be considered when evaluating Paul's theology in order to ensure that we don't, as Peter says, "*distort*" Paul's writings or any other scripture. Perhaps I shouldn't; but, I find a small encouragement in the fact that even Peter said that Paul's writings "*contain some things that are hard to understand*". Hopefully, by using scripture to interpret scripture we will be able to properly discern the meaning of many key phrases in the Pauline epistles. I couldn't emphasize enough the need to grasp the manner in which the "history book of the Church" displays the Torah or Law. At the risk of boring you, I want to share a couple more examples from the book of Acts before moving on.

Acts 25:8
8 Then Paul made his defense: "**I have done nothing wrong against the law of the Jews** or against the temple or against Caesar."

When you begin to "string" these passages together they paint a rather vivid picture of believing Jews including Paul who are/were:

- Acts 21:20 "zealous for the Law"
- Acts 21:24 "living in obedience to the Law"
- Acts 22:12 "devout observer*(s)* of the Law"
- Acts 24:14 "*in* agree(*ment*) with the Law
- Acts 24:17 "ceremonially clean"

Finally, in *Acts 25:8* Paul makes the statement that he had "*done nothing wrong against the law of the Jews.*" Personally, I am very glad that he added the words "*of the Jews*" since some systems of interpretation work very hard to make the word "Law" mean something other than what the readers would obviously understand it to mean… **Torah**" The historical record is patently clear regarding how even the "Apostle to the Gentiles" viewed the Law or Torah. This fact forces me to ask why I missed what is blatant for so long. **I believe that it is because I threw out the "baby" (Law) with the "bath water" (curse of the Law).** On the note of examples from Acts that I (and possibly you) have overlooked or not fully appreciated in the past, read the following scripture and ask yourself if Paul was lying or telling the truth:

Acts 23:6
6 Then Paul, knowing that some of them were Sadducees and the others Pharisees, called out in the Sanhedrin, "My brothers, **I am a Pharisee**, the son of a Pharisee. I stand on trial because of my hope in the resurrection of the dead."

Paul did not say I **was** a Pharisee. He said, "**I am a Pharisee**." I disregarded the truth of Paul's plain statement for years as a mere tactic to influence his trial. This idea is really foolish for a myriad of reasons but suffice it to say that Paul was no liar.

The book of Acts clearly reveals the nature of Paul's love for and observance of the Torah. *Acts 13, Acts 14, Acts 17, Acts 18*, and *Acts 19* all contain accounts of Paul and his companions during his first and second missionary journeys observing Sabbath by attending synagogue. Luke even records the words, "*as was his custom*" and "*as usual*" when referring to going to the synagogue on the Sabbath. What is more amazing and usually overlooked is that they were initially welcomed **and usually asked to speak**. This could only be because they were perceived by the Jewish community as Torah observant. One possible explanation for Paul repeatedly being asked to speak is that he was viewed as a Pharisee. This agrees with Paul's own words and with the customs of the day in which Pharisees from Jerusalem were invited to teach among Diaspora Jews (Jews scattered among Gentile nations).

As we leave the book of Acts let me point out a couple of other things worth considering. In *Acts 10*, Peter had to be told (by God) **3 times** to kill and eat something in a vision that was not kosher; his reluctance had to be because Peter had been keeping the dietary laws (many years after the resurrection). **Thus it would not be unreasonable to conclude that Peter didn't understand Jesus to be abolishing even the dietary law!** Additionally, Peter understood the point of the vision to relate to fellowshipping with Gentiles. Although the Law did not make a prohibition against fellowshipping with Gentiles the Jews of Jesus' day taught in "Halakah" (their tradition of the right way to walk with God and interpret the Law) that you couldn't fellowship with Gentiles for fear that you would become ceremonially unclean if they had eaten something non-kosher. The Holy Spirit used Peter's vision to correct this miss-application of the Law. In *Acts 11,* Peter felt it was necessary to explain his actions to the community of believers. **This could only be because the community of believers or early church was keeping kosher (many years after the resurrection) and had not understood Jesus to have abolished even the dietary law!** *Acts 11:18* indicates that the early church accepted the Holy Spirit's guidance given to Peter regarding <u>the right way to relate to the Law</u>. In other words the believing Jews of the early church were keeping the dietary law. Furthermore, they were holding to what the Jews call "Halakah" which said that they had to go beyond what was written in the Law and not even enter a Gentile's house. The Holy Spirit corrected this miss-application of the Law and better yet showed them the <u>proper way</u> to "Halakah" or walk with God. This is reminiscent of two things that we will discuss later. **First**, that the Jewish nation was waiting for the Holy Spirit to move them to understand and keep the Law to the point that it would be written on their hearts (***Ezek 36:26-27***). **Second**, that Jesus began this process in his ministry by saying things like: You have heard it said, 'Do not murder' but I tell you… You have heard it said, 'Do not commit adultery' but I tell you… <u>All of these statements took the Law which was right and expounded upon</u> **its righteous intentions** showing the right way to "Halakah". I am convinced that a careful examination of almost every encounter Jesus had with a religious leader will reveal Jesus showing them <u>the proper way to relate to the existing Law</u>! This will be discussed more as we cover *Matthew 5* in later paragraphs. As we close the discussion on the book of Acts, please take note that **Peter, James, Ananias, Paul, and the whole community of believers were living in what they considered obedience to the Law as** (I believe) motivated **and led by the Spirit rather than fear of a penalty or curse.** In the closing paragraphs of Acts we find the words,

"*...he explained and declared to them the kingdom of God and tried to convince them about Jesus **from the Law of Moses**...*" The conclusion that you are forced to reach after reviewing the book of Acts is that Paul and the other believers loved the Torah. They considered themselves as living in obedience to Law. The book of Acts covers approximately 30 years of history following Jesus' earthly ministry and yet the Torah observance of Jewish believers including Paul, Peter, James, Ananias, and the community of believers at Jerusalem is demonstrated throughout the book. What I mean is this: Acts gives us a picture of the Messianic believers observing the Law consistently over a 30 year period, not some brief transitional period. Don't we do ourselves a great injustice if we fail to consider this when reading the Pauline epistles! Would we approach any other issue in the scripture with such reckless indifference for the **clear historical record of the practice of the Apostles**? If Paul thought the Law was only a restraint and a bondage, why did he still consider himself a Pharisee and a Torah-observant Jew? **Please consider the possibility that we may have over emphasized one facet of the multifaceted Law to the point that we have erred!**

****Let me at this juncture again take the opportunity to alleviate any concerns welling up within you regarding "Judaizing". I am a Gentile believer who has entered into covenant with God by way of faith in Jesus. I rely on the empowerment of the Holy Spirit, the **whole** counsel of the Word of God, the growing and abiding faith within me, the work of Jesus on the Cross, the power of the resurrection, and the mercy and grace found in the gospel for salvation! I haven't even been compelled to circumcise my own sons...This ought to lay to rest any questions about Judaizing.*

A Theological Foundation

At this point hopefully you (along with me) are at least reconsidering the validity of some of your previously held views. However, words from Galatians, Romans, or possibly Hebrews are no doubt streaming through your mind warring against the acceptance of any new ideas in this arena. I promise I empathize with the difficulty of reconciling the clear historical testimony from the book of Acts with many of the statements in the epistles. I will do my best to lend insight to many of those passages, but first I think it is necessary to review what the Tanakh (Older Testament) says about the Torah (Law) that lies within it. When reading a lengthy paper like this one, there is often a temptation is "skim over" the scriptural quotations because they are somewhat familiar. **Please do not do that in this instance! You owe it to yourself to read the references below even when they seem repetitious.** This will give you a sense of the biblical view of the Torah to bring into balance our understanding of the Law. My hope is that we will come to a balance in our view of the Law that both acknowledges its **limitations** and also recognizes its **benefits**.

Deut 13:1-5
13:1 If a prophet, or one who foretells by dreams, appears among you and announces to you a miraculous sign or wonder, 2 **and if the sign or wonder of which he has spoken takes place, and he says, "Let us follow other gods" (gods you have not known) "and let us worship them,"** 3 you must not listen to the words of that prophet or dreamer. **The LORD your God is testing you to find out whether you love him with all your heart and with all your soul. 4 It is the LORD your God you must follow, and him you must revere. Keep his commands and obey him; serve

him and hold fast to him. 5 That prophet or dreamer must be put to death, because he preached rebellion against the LORD your God, who brought you out of Egypt and redeemed you from the land of slavery; he has tried to turn you from **the way the LORD your God commanded you to follow**. You must purge the evil from among you.

One of the more important things that I hope you will grasp from this passage is that **the Law formed a theological foundation for the Jewish people**. In the passage above, Israel was told that even a *real* prophet or miracle worker that performed signs but advocated following other gods or tried to *"turn you from the way the LORD your God commanded you"* was to be stoned. The words *"Keep his commands and obey him..."* from verse **4**, sum up *"the way the LORD your God commanded you to follow"!* The importance of this passage can't be over looked. If *real* miracle workers and prophets came to a Jew but advocated something other than the Law, the Bible forbids them to follow that "new/strange way". In case you are tempted to believe that the commands being referenced are something other than the Law; consider the context. This chapter is in the middle of the Law and the word for commands is "Mitzvah" which refers to the commands within the Law. The rest of ***Deuteronomy 13*** goes on to suggest that even fellow Israelites or family members that try to *"turn you from the way the LORD your God commanded you"* were to be shown no mercy. Given this fact, it is fair to say that **the Torah (Including the Law) formed the first foundational revelation given to Israel and all other revelation would be evaluated based on its continuity with the Law.** This means that when the books of Isaiah, Jeremiah, or Ezekiel were being considered to determine if they were scripture, the standard was the Torah! The Torah certainly wasn't comprehensive or else there would not have been a need for any of the other scripture; however, the other scripture could not contradict the Torah because it is/was the standard. Each successive revelation built upon the previous to form a **unified revelation of God**! This building process formed an ever-increasingly clearer picture of who God is and how to relate to Him. So then, Jeremiah may contain revelation in addition to the Torah but not revelation opposed to the Torah. <u>Likewise, the epistles may contain revelation in addition to the Torah but not revelation opposed to the Torah or it would not be scripture!</u> This fact should cause you (as it did me) serious concern if you have held a view that suggests that any part of the Newer Testament was opposed to the Law. Perhaps this is why Jesus, Paul, James, Ananias, and the community of believers at Jerusalem never departed from being Torah-observant. Before moving on, I can't help but ask if you noticed the similarity between verses *3-4* and *1 John 5:2-3*? Both passages equate keeping the "*commands*" with loving God. Let's move on to the Psalms to get an idea of how the Law is presented. *(Again, I remind you of the need to **actually and fully** read each of these passages—the repetition is intentional)*

Ps 1:1-3
Blessed is the man
who does not walk in the counsel of the wicked
or stand in the way of sinners
or sit in the seat of mockers.
2 But **his delight is in the law of the LORD, and on his law he meditates day and night**.
3 He is like a tree planted by streams of water,
which <u>yields its fruit</u> in season
and whose leaf does not wither.
<u>Whatever he does prospers.</u>

Contrary to the idea that the Law is bondage, slavery, and a burden this Psalm presents the Law as a "*delight*". The Word of God contained in this

Psalm encourages the reader to meditate day and night on the *"law of the LORD"*. Additionally, the writer indicates that this will *"yield(s) it(s) fruit in season"* which is something I know every serious Christian wants to do. (Incidentally, the Septuagint uses the word "Nomos" for Law here but the Hebrew is "Torah"…I say this only to help you avoid making the mistake of thinking that "law" only refers to instruction and not what it obviously means "the divine instruction contained in the Torah". The original writer and reader had the Law contained in the Torah in view.)

Ps 19:7-14
7 The law of the LORD is perfect, reviving the soul. The <u>statutes</u> of the LORD are <u>trustworthy</u>, making wise the simple. 8 The <u>precepts</u> of the LORD are right, giving joy to the heart. The <u>commands</u> of the LORD are radiant, giving light to the eyes. 9 The fear of the LORD is pure, enduring forever. The <u>ordinances</u> of the LORD are sure and **altogether righteous**. 10 **They are more precious than gold, than much pure gold; they are sweeter than honey, than honey from the comb. 11 By them is your servant warned; in keeping them there is great reward.**
12 Who can discern his errors? Forgive my hidden faults. 13 Keep your servant also <u>from willful sins; may they not rule over me</u>. Then will I be blameless, innocent of great transgression.
14 May the words of my mouth and the meditation of my heart be pleasing in your sight, O LORD, my Rock and my Redeemer.

This Psalm covers all the bases of possible errors in misinterpretation. The *"law of the LORD…statutes of the LORD…commands of the LORD…ordinances of the LORD are…altogether righteous."* No matter how a predisposition against the Law might tempt a person to re-interpret the words *"Nomos, Torah,* law, or Law" this Psalm is clear! The words: **perfect, trustworthy, right, radiant, pure, sure,**

and righteous are all used to describe the Law. Further more, the Law is said to:
- *"revive(ing) the soul"*
- *"make(ing) wise the simple"*
- *"give(ing) joy to the heart"*
- *"give(ing) light to the eyes"*

Are these phrases that you would be comfortable using to describe the Mosaic Law? We have no problem applying these phrases to the "Word" as a whole, but some recoil when trying to apply these phrases to the Mosaic Law; Why? **Statutes, commands, ordinances, are all words that certainly refer to the Mosaic Law.** In light of the clear historical testimony found in the book of Acts as Christians we must ask ourselves if Paul, James, Peter, Ananias and the Jerusalem Elders would have had any such reservations. Perhaps we have thrown out the "baby" (**Law**) with the "bath water" (**curses of the Law**). ***I am taking another opportunity to ask for your patience in getting to the Pauline epistles. I think it is advantageous for us to get a taste of the theological foundation that the Apostles had before interpreting their writings.

Ps 94:12
12 Blessed is the man you discipline, O LORD, the **man you teach from your law**

Most Christians have no problem with the idea that the Law disciplines. In fact, we have emphasized that point until we *only* see the Law as a harsh disciplinarian and cruel supervisor. The curses prescribed in the Law certainly functioned as a harsh disciplinarian and "supervised" (I promise to discuss this in Galatians) but that was not the only role! Look at the scripture above, *"the man you teach from your law"*. The Law also functioned as a teacher that: **revived the soul, made wise the simple, gave joy to the heart, gave light to the eyes, was a delight, caused the recipients to bear**

18

fruit in season, and prosper. There is not one item in the preceding list that did not come directly out of the preceding scriptures. Remember, my goal is to bring into focus a biblically balanced view of the Law. Most of us understand the Law's role as a disciplinarian but few of us have properly emphasized the Law as a trainer of righteousness *(2 Tim 3:16)*. This lack of understanding of the positive aspects of the Law could be very damaging if Gentile believers hope to arouse envy in Israel. It may even cause otherwise receptive Israelites to be repulsed. What is worse…you may be missing the fullness and richness of the Word of God. Are you surprised at the positive things said to come from the Law? Maybe we have "stereotyped" the Law in only one vein and have therefore missed out on the "*delight*(ful)" aspects of the Law. The next Psalm I quote from is one that really should be read in its entirety; but for brevity's sake, I excerpt it here. (Please don't skip ahead…the Apostles had this taught to them from birth and could quote this from memory)

Ps 119:1
Blessed are they whose ways are blameless,
who walk according to the law of the LORD.

Perhaps this is why the early believers didn't see observing the Law as contrary to faith.

Ps 119:18
18 Open my eyes that I may see
wonderful things in your law .

This has really become my prayer! I want to see the "*wonderful things in your law*" Lord. Even people that have served Jesus for years may benefit from having their "eyes" opened to the "*wonderful things in*" the Law. Our incorrect "stereotyping" of the

Law as solely restrictive has prevented us from seeing the *"wonderful things"* in the Law.

Ps 119:20
20 My soul is consumed **with longing for your laws** at all times.

This beautiful Psalm was arranged in a way to aide with memory. It utilizes literary devices to evoke emotion and assist in memorization. I lack the ability to describe the way in which a national Hebrew would read this Psalm; but one thing is very clear, **the Psalm portrays the Law as invigorating as opposed to oppressive!** Verse 20 speaks of being consumed with longing for the Law. This is similar to the love I have for Jesus! I personally believe that this is because the Law displays the righteous character of God and so those who love Him were consumed with a love for the Law. While the Law accurately displays the character of God, Jesus is the perfect embodiment and *fullest* revelation of the character of God. <u>So then while I am thrilled with the Law…I am enthralled with Jesus.</u> This doesn't diminish the Law; you might even say Jesus magnifies the Law as its perfect representation or its goal. An analogy may be that the Torah is a "novel" about the character of God but Jesus is the "major motion picture" based on the "novel".

Ps 119:33-37
Teach me, O LORD, **to follow your decrees**; then I will keep them to the end.
34 Give me understanding, and **I will keep your law** and obey it with all my heart.
35 Direct me **in the path of your commands**, for there I find delight.
36 **Turn my heart toward your statutes** and not toward selfish gain.
37 Turn my eyes away from worthless things;

preserve my life according to your word.

The cry of the Psalmist is not for the abolishment of the Law, but rather the power and understanding to relate properly to it. Notice the requests: *"Teach me", "Give me understanding", "Direct me",* and *"Turn my heart".* Are these not all things that the Holy Spirit does for believers regarding the Word? Doesn't He teach us, give us understanding, direct us, and turn our hearts toward Holy things? **The problem was never with the Law…the problem was always with the people!** The law was spiritual but they were unspiritual *(Rom 7:14).* I will get into this problem and solution soon but for now finish reading the Psalm.

Ps 119:41-48
May your unfailing love come to me, O LORD,
your salvation according to your promise;
42 then I will answer the one who taunts me,
for I trust in your word.
43 Do not snatch the word of truth from my mouth,
for **I have put my hope in your laws**.
44 **I will always obey your law, for ever and ever.**
45 **I will walk about in freedom,**
for I have sought out your precepts.
46 I will speak of your statutes before kings
and will not be put to shame,
47 for **I delight in your commands because I love them**.
48 I lift up my hands to your commands, which I love, and **I meditate on your decrees.**

The Psalmist says, *"I trust in your word…Do not snatch the word of truth from my mouth…"* What word is he talking about? The answer is in verse **43** and **44**. *"…I have put my **hope in your laws**. I will always **obey your law**, for ever and ever."* The most profound part of this section of the Psalm (to me) is in verses **45 "I will walk about in freedom,**

for I have sought out your precepts." For years I only viewed the Law as restrictive and bondage. This Psalm seems to clearly portray an additional but not contrary point of view. The Psalmist clearly says that he will walk in freedom because of the precepts, but that doesn't mean that these same laws were not bondage to other people. When my wife and I established a budget for the very first time, she saw it as freedom and I saw it as bondage. She saw what she was free to spend; I only saw what I could not do! **The Law displays the good that believers are free to do**! Perhaps this is what James was referring to when he wrote, *"But the man who looks intently into the perfect law that gives freedom, and continues to do this, not forgetting what he has heard, but doing it — he will be blessed in what he does."* or *"Speak and act as those who are going to be judged by the law that gives freedom"* My negative views of the Law had always forced an alternate interpretation, but now I can't help but see these words in the light of the similar language throughout the Psalms. This fact is even more powerful if you consider that James remained a Torah-observant Jew who undoubtedly had this Psalm memorized from early childhood. In addition to pointing out our sin, the Law is clearly described as promoting freedom. *(Don't give up…read the rest of these quotes, the repetition will help to erode false precepts)*

Ps 119:72
72 The **law from your mouth is more precious** to me than thousands of pieces of silver and gold.

Ps 119:77
77 Let your compassion come to me that I may live, for **your law is my delight**.

Ps 119:97-103
Oh, how **I love your law!**
I meditate on it all day long.
98 **Your commands make me wiser** than my enemies, for they are ever with me.
99 I have more insight than all my teachers, for **I meditate on your statutes**.
100 I have more understanding than the elders, for **I obey your precepts**.
101 I have kept my feet from every evil path so that I might obey your word.
102 **I have not departed from your laws,** for you yourself have taught me.
103 **How sweet are your words to my taste.**
104 I **gain understanding from your precepts**; therefore I hate every wrong path.
105 **Your word is a lamp to my feet and a light for my path.**
106 **I have taken an oath and confirmed it, that I will follow your righteous laws**.
107 I have suffered much; preserve my life, O LORD, according to your word.
108 Accept, O LORD, the willing praise of my mouth, **and teach me your laws**.

When I was first Spirit-filled, I used to walk and pray on my lunch and coffee breaks. One of my favorite songs to sing, while focusing on Jesus, went like this:

Jesus, Holy and anointed one…Your name is like honey on my lips and you word is a lamp unto my feet…

I never really thought about where the song may have been derived. Years later, while reading the Psalms, it dawned on me that the "word" spoken of in the Psalms as a lamp, sweet to the taste, etc. was the Law. At the time the majority of Psalms were written, the Torah was the only thing in existence! I don't say this to take away from the idea that Jesus is all of those things; after all, He is the perfect representation of the character of God found in the Law. Next time you sing "Lord you are more precious than silver…" perhaps it will remind you of verse **72** *"The **law from your mouth is more precious** to me than thousands of pieces of silver and gold"*. A clearer more balanced view of the Law should be coming into focus at this point…Remember the passages you are reading formed the Apostles theological foundation.

Ps 119:142-144
142 **Your righteousness is everlasting and your law is true**.
143 Trouble and distress have come upon me, but your commands are my delight.
144 Your statutes are forever right; give me understanding that I may live.

Ps 119:162-168
162 I rejoice in your promise like one who finds great spoil.
163 I hate and abhor falsehood but **I love your law**.
164 **Seven times a day I praise you for your righteous laws**.
165 Great **peace** **have they who love your law**, and nothing can make them stumble.
166 I wait for your salvation, O LORD,
and **I follow your commands**.
167 **I obey your statutes**, for **I love them greatly**.
168 I obey your precepts and your statutes, for all my ways are known to you.

As the Lord opens our eyes to the wonderful things in His Law, We will be able to say with joy, *"Seven times a day I praise you for your righteous laws."* One more noteworthy theological point before leaving the Psalms is illustrated in **Verses 166-168**.

The writer says, "*I will **wait for your salvation**, O LORD, **and** I will follow your commands...*" The Law was never meant to be a source of salvation!!! The writer said "*I will wait for your salvation...and I will follow your commands...*" **The proper relationship to the Law was not as a means of salvation, but rather instructions on a right way to live!** I believe most of the seemingly negative statements concerning the Law in the Pauline epistles are directed towards an attitude that perverted the Torah into a means of salvation rather than instructions on how to live. This was never the intent of the Torah, but was prevalent in 1st century Israel. If my premise is right, that would explain how the Apostles could love the Law and yet work to tear down a perverted, false application of it. **The Law was not meant to compete with Jesus; it was meant to magnify Him!** Today in our churches few people are trusting in the Mosaic Law for salvation! How could they? They don't even know what it says. The veracity with which some of the epistles attack the perversion of the Torah into a means of salvation was proportional to the audience's propensity to utilize the Torah falsely as a means of salvation. It is not uncommon to make a very strong statement to the right in the hope of bringing someone who is out of balance to the left back to the middle, but if that same strong statement is given to someone who is out of balance to the right...the result is someone out of balance to the right! In other words, if the same strong statements in the epistles used to correct a group of people who were **relying on the Law as a means of salvation** are then applied to a people with the opposite inclination, the result may be that you end up with a people that have **no regard for the Law**. Might this be at least part of the reason we have failed to see the "*wonderful things*" found in the Law? We will leave the Psalms with this last quotation:

Ps 119:174-176
174 **I long for your salvation**, O LORD, *and* **your law is my delight**.
175 Let me live that I may praise you, and **may your laws sustain me**.
176 I have strayed like a lost sheep.
Seek your servant, for I have not forgotten **your commands**.

The scripture above echoes the idea that **salvation** and **obedience to the Law** are completely separate issues. You might paraphrase the sentiment expressed in the scripture by saying: I wait for your salvation Lord and I delight in the righteousness revealed in your Law because it sustains me while I wait. Shortly, we will leave the Tanakh (Older Testament) and venture back into the Newer Testament. Prior to leaving the Tanakh, it would be beneficial for us to closely examine two important prophecies. The first is found in ***Jeremiah 31***. In its context, this scripture is referring to a time when the curses of the Law had fallen upon Israel. In the later portions of the book of Deuteronomy curses were pronounced on Israel if they broke the covenant God was giving them. Jeremiah begins by telling them what will happen in the future after they had endured this punishment. Jeremiah begins by telling them a *"time is coming"*:

Jer 31:31-37
31 "The time is coming," declares the LORD, "when I will make a **new covenant with the house of Israel and with the house of Judah**. 32 It will not be like the covenant I made with their forefathers when I took them by the hand to lead them out of Egypt, because **they broke my covenant**, though I was a husband to them," declares the LORD.

The first couple verses refer to a principle that I have eluded to already but that is worth restating. The problem with the Older Covenant was that they broke it. The promises of the covenant were **good**, the precepts of the covenant were **righteous**, the statues of the covenant were all together **lovely**…the problem was not with the covenant, it was with the people's inability to keep the covenant. The solution is found in the following verses:

33 "This is the covenant I will make with the house of Israel after that time," declares the LORD."**I will put my law in their minds and write it on their hearts**. I will be their God, and they will be my people. 34 No longer will a man teach his neighbor, or a man his brother, saying, 'Know the LORD, 'because they will all know me, from the least of them to the greatest," declares the LORD. "For **I will forgive their wickedness and will remember their sins no more**."

The problem was that the people, as a whole, were unable to keep the covenant because of the weakness of their sinful nature. To resolve the problem, God promised to impress his Law on their minds and impress his Law on their hearts. This is not unlike what the Psalmist cried out for when he said: *"**Teach me**, O LORD, to follow your decrees; then I will keep them to the end. **Give me understanding**, and I will keep your law and obey it with all my heart. **Direct me** in the path of your commands, for there I find delight. **Turn my heart** toward your statutes and not toward selfish gain. **Turn my eyes away from worthless things;** preserve my life according to your word."* The Law contained in the covenant was good, righteous, and spiritual *(Rom 7:12)* but the problem was that the sinful nature of the people kept them from obeying it *(Rom 8:3)*. They needed new hearts,

understanding, and eyes! All of these things are
found in the empowerment of the Holy Spirit.
Jeremiah was not so much describing a completely
new covenant as he was describing a completely
new way to relate to the existing covenant. We will
get to that in Ezekiel, but first let's finish Jeremiah
and see what he says about the **enduring Law**.

Jeremiah 31:35
35 This is what the LORD says,
he who appoints the sun to shine by day, who
decrees the moon and stars to shine by night, who
stirs up the sea so that its waves roar — the LORD
Almighty is his name: 36 "**Only if these decrees
vanish from my sight**, "declares the LORD, "**will
the descendants of Israel ever cease to be a
nation before me.**"
37 This is what the LORD says:
"**Only if the heavens above can be measured and
the foundations of the earth below be searched
out will I reject all the descendants of Israel
because of all they have done**," declares the
LORD."

We will move on to Ezekiel but I felt it necessary
(although redundant) to point out that verses **36-37**
declare that the "*decrees*" and the people **will
coexist forever**. The nation of Israel's existence is
a divine endorsement of the Law and the Law is a
divine endorsement of the nation of Israel. Please
take note of one last thing before moving on to
Ezekiel. The primary change in the Newer
Covenant according to Jeremiah is the way the
people relate to the Law. **It would be internally
motivated rather than externally motivated.** I
think that Ezekiel will make this point clearer by
pointing out that the ministry of the Holy Spirit will
motivate the people to keep the Law, rather than,
their motivation coming from a curse or penalty of
the Law (which is removed in Christ). The context

28

for this passage is the same as the Jeremiah passage we've just discussed. Israel has experienced the curses written about in the Law as a result of the weakness of their sinful nature and the prophecy concerns a time when Israel would be restored, cleansed, and given God's Holy Spirit as an empowerment to keep the Law. The problem is that the Law was weakened through the sinful nature and the solution would not be to dismantle the Law…it would be to further empower the people and at the same time cleanse them.

Ezek 36:23-29
23 I will show the holiness of my great name, which has been profaned among the nations, the name you have profaned among them. Then the nations will know that I am the LORD, declares the Sovereign LORD, when **I show myself holy through you before their eyes.**

24 "'For I will take you out of the nations; I will gather you from all the countries and bring you back into your own land. 25 I will **sprinkle clean water on you, and you will be clean**; I will cleanse you from all your impurities and from all your idols. **26 I will give you a new heart and put a new spirit in you; I will remove from you your heart of stone and give you a heart of flesh. 27 And I will put my Spirit in you and move you to follow my decrees and be careful to keep my laws.** 28 You will live in the land I gave your forefathers; you will be my people, and I will be your God. 29 **I will save you from all your uncleanness.**

This powerful passage addresses the heart of the issue, in that, the Law is righteous but men are not! (*Rom 7:12-14*) Therefore, no one can be justified by the Law. (*Rom 3:28*) The inability to be justified by the Law does not mean that the Law is bad, useless, or inoperative. It means that we, in and of ourselves, are woefully inadequate. The flaw in the Mosaic covenant was the unspiritual human failings that demanded a penalty—the curses of the Law and Death! (***Rom 6:23***). While the Law beautifully displays the righteous character of God, it also reveals the ugly inadequacies of unspiritual man. The divine solution was that God would show Himself as holy through Israel by **cleansing them (grace)**, **giving them new hearts (faith)**, and **empowering them** with the Holy Spirit to "*follow…and keep* (the) *laws*". This is not the abolishment of the Law; it is the fulfillment of the Law. Thus, our trust in Him or faith in Him doesn't nullify the Law; but rather, it upholds it. *(Rom 3:31)* We no longer relate to the Law as a fearful task-master ready to punish our disobedience. Instead we joyfully embrace the righteousness found within the Law as empowered by God's Holy Spirit. Every area of short coming revealed by the Law in us is covered by grace through faith in what Jesus did when "Christ *redeemed us from the **curse of the law** by becoming a curse for us*". Ezekiel foresaw this when he said, God would "s*ave you from all your uncleanness."* This is also how it can be said that someone is not under the Law (its penalty), but is also not free from God's Law (its righteous requirements).

The Apostles had a rich theological foundation to draw from concerning the Law. I am optimistic that you are beginning to see the positive attributes displayed in the Law. When we move into the Newer Testament it is very important that you consider the following points that I have tried to make:

Historical record of the Apostles' view of the Law	**Acts 10 & 11** – Peter and the community of believers are keeping kosher yet receptive to the Holy Spirit's direction regarding how they related to the Law
	Acts 13, 14, 17, 18, 19 – records Paul and his companions as observing Sabbath in Synagogues. Luke often adds "as was his custom"
	Acts 21:20 – Thousands of believing Jews are "zealous for the Law"
	Acts 21:24 – Paul deliberately proves himself to be "living in obedience to the Law"
	Acts 22:12 – Ananias was a believer and a "devout observer of the Law"
	Acts 23:6 – Paul calls himself a Pharisee (in the present tense)
	Acts 24:14 – Paul was in "agreement with the Law"
	Acts 24:17 – Paul was found to be "ceremonially clean"
	Acts 28:23 – 30 years after Jesus' resurrection, Paul met with the leader of the Jews and "tried to convince them about Jesus from the Law of Moses..."
Older Testament view of the Torah (Law) A Theological Foundation	**Deut 13:1-5** – The Law is the measuring stick for all future revelation even if delivered by prophets and miracle workers
	Ps 1:2 – The Law is not burdensome it is a "delight" and something to be "meditated on day and night"
	Ps 17:7-10 – Far from oppressive, the Law is "perfect", "reviving the soul", "altogether righteous", "giving joy to the heart", "more precious than gold", and "sweeter than honey"
	Ps 94:12 – The Law had definite teaching aspects "Blessed is the man you discipline… the man you teach from your law"
	Ps 119:1 – "Blessed are they… who walk according to the law of the LORD"
	Ps 119:18-20 – The "wonderful things" in the Law created a "longing" for the (Law) that consumed the Psalmist
	Ps 119:33-37 – The Psalmist acknowledged his need for a better way to relate to the Law *"Teach me"*, *"Give me understanding"*, *"Direct me"*, and *"Turn my heart"* In effect he was asking for the Holy Spirit empowerment.
	Ps 119:41-48 – The Law is a source of hope and freedom
	Jer 31:31-37 – the "Newer Covenant" would place the Law in the mind and write it on the heart rather than abolish it.
	Ezek 36:27 – The LORD would "put my Spirit in you and move you to follow my decrees and be careful to keep my laws."

Dispensational Segmentation or "Unbroken" Promises

Now that our discussion has returned to the Newer Testament, there may be a subtle inclination to divorce the theological foundation found in the Older Testament from the Newer scriptures. I ask you to remember ***Deuteronomy 13*** which teaches that Israel could not accept any revelation that was inconsistent with what God had already given them in the Law. The terms "Old" and "New" suggest that the "Old" is defunct and replaced by the "New". This simply can not be the case! James makes it clear that "*...the Father...does not change like shifting shadows*". The cannon of Scripture is composed of the foundational revelation in the Torah and the successive inspired writings. These additional writings further the original revelation but **can not contradict** it. Look at the words of Jesus regarding the ***continuity*** of the Scripture. The context of these verses relates to a debate over whether or not it is *scriptural* for Jesus to claim to be "*God's Son*".

John 10:35-36
35 If he called them 'gods,' to whom the word of God came — and **the Scripture cannot be broken**— 36 what about the one whom the Father set apart as his very own and sent into the world? Why then do you accuse me of blasphemy because I said, 'I am God's Son'

Jesus, Himself, said that the scripture ***could not be broken***! Please read the Amplified's rendering of the same scripture. (I have not edited or altered the wording or formatting in this verse)

35 So men are called gods [by the Law], men to whom God's message came — and the Scripture cannot be set aside or cancelled or broken or annulled —AMP

The undeniable conclusion, by Jesus own words, is that the Older Testament is not **set aside, cancelled, broken, or annulled.** The very heart and foundation of the Older Testament is the Torah and the center of the Torah is the Mosaic Law. The very scripture that promises a Newer Covenant in *Jeremiah 31*, also affirms that the decrees (Laws) would never cease and would coexist with Israel forever. Torah-observant Jews (especially of the Pharisaic order "like Paul") viewed the Torah as the first in a contiguous series of unified, inspired writings. Perhaps this is why Jesus said the following:

Matt 5:17-19
17 "Do not think that I have come to abolish the Law or the Prophets; **I have not come to abolish them but to fulfill them.** 18 I tell you the truth, <u>until heaven and earth disappear</u>, not the smallest letter, not the least stroke of a pen, **will by any means disappear from the Law** until everything is accomplished. 19 Anyone who breaks one of the least of these commandments and teaches others to do the same will be called least in the kingdom of heaven, but **whoever practices and teaches these commands will be called great in the kingdom of heaven.**

The historical testimony displayed in the practice of the Apostles and recorded in the book of Acts, overwhelmingly, confirms that Jesus' followers understood the words above. Peter, James, Paul, Ananias, the Jerusalem Elders, and the thousands of Jews in the community of believers **can all be positively identified as observing the Law.** An interpretation of the text above that renders this statement as "transitional" or otherwise "inapplicable" to believers today is at the very least *forced* and at the very most a complete *bastardization* of the text. Sound biblical interpretation always views an individual scripture in the "light" of the larger volume of scripture. This means that Deuteronomy, Jeremiah, Ezekiel, hundreds of Psalms, and the entire Tanakh has to be considered when interpreting Jesus' words. Additionally, within this passage of scripture the following statement is made:

18"I tell you the truth, **until heaven and earth disappear**, not the smallest letter, not the least stroke of a pen, **will by any means disappear from the Law** until everything is accomplished"

Every manipulation of the text imaginable can not make "*heaven and earth disappear*" which is the stated requirement for the Law to disappear. I want to confess, I have often misinterpreted this passage. I sought to blunt the obvious endorsement of the Law because it was inconsistent with my misunderstanding of the Pauline epistles. As usual, the problem was not with the epistles or Jesus' words; the problem was with me! My narrow view of only one of the facets of the Law (its restrictiveness) precluded me from seeing the many "*wonderful things*" in the Law. Praise be to God for working patiently with fools (you may be thinking I am a fool on multiple levels at this point). Many well meaning people have used the phrase "*…until everything is accomplished*" to render the Law as inoperative. Their basic line of thought is that Jesus finished His earthly ministry with the words, "*…it is finished*" and so the Law is therefore no longer applicable to believers. The obvious problem with this line of thought is that "*heaven and earth* (didn't) *disappear*". One of the **more convicting**

thoughts that I have had in years was that I may have been guilty of making the same kind of argument that is used by some to render the Spiritual Gifts obsolete and inoperative. In the early years of my Christian walk, a powerful man of God freed me from the misapplication of *1 Corinthians 13:10* which used the phrase "*...when perfection comes, the imperfect disappears...*" to say that the Spiritual Gifts had passed away. Once freed from the error of misinterpretation, a whole new blessing in the scriptures was available to me. I pray with all of my heart that I am able to impart some bit of wisdom that will allow you to be opened to the blessings **that come from a Biblically-balanced view of the Law**.

Internal and External Motivation

Matthew 5:19
19 Anyone who breaks one of the least of these commandments and teaches others to do the same will be called least in the kingdom of heaven, but **whoever practices and teaches these commands will be called great in the kingdom of heaven.**

Notice that Jesus did not say that someone *"who breaks...these commandments"* will be **cursed by the Law, killed, or damned.** In the Newer Covenant the *"curses of the Law"* have been laid upon Jesus, and just like in the Older Covenant...Salvation is an act of grace appropriated through trust in God. Salvation has never been by a system of works. Jesus did say that the one *"who breaks...these commandments"* would be *"least in the kingdom of Heaven"*. The phrase *"...least in the kingdom of heaven"* is set in opposition to the phrase*"...great in the kingdom of heaven"*. Jesus was not advocating salvation through the Law because that was never the Law's purpose. Jesus was endorsing the righteous intentions of the Law as rewarding way to live. The theological foundation that the Apostles had said that the Law was: **perfect, trustworthy, right, radiant, pure, sure, and righteous** (these scriptures were previously quoted). Therefore, the Law was not a means of salvation...it was a righteous way to live while waiting for salvation to be revealed. In *Psalm 119*, the Psalmist asked for God to: teach him, guide him, direct him, and turn him. In context, all of these requests were made regarding the right way to relate to the Law. The Psalmist wanted God: **to teach him the Law, guide him in the Law, direct him in the Law,** and **turn him towards the Law**

and away from wickedness. His conclusion was that if these things were done, he would be able to "*keep them*(the laws) *to the end*" and "*obey it with all my*(his) *hear*t". The Psalmist was, in a manner of speaking, asking for the indwelling of the Holy Spirit. He went on to say it would then be a "*delight*" to him. Much in the same way "Spirit-Led" believers today find doing God's Will a delight! Immediately after Jesus said "*I have not come to abolish them* (the laws) *but to fulfill them...not the least stroke of a pen, will by any means disappear from the Law...whoever practices and teaches these commands will be called great in the kingdom of heaven*", He went on to teach, guide, direct, and turn them towards the righteous intentions and proper interpretation of the Law. *Matthew 5:21* starts with a series of statements that are typical of Jesus' teachings.

Matt 5:21-22
.21 "You have heard that it was said to the people long ago, 'Do not murder, and anyone who murders will be subject to judgment.' 22 But I tell you that anyone who is angry with his brother will be subject to judgment.

This is one of hundreds of examples where Jesus gave Israel the proper interpretation of the Law. He **taught them, guided them, directed them, and turned them** towards the righteous intentions in the Law. Nearly every conversation that Jesus had with the religious leaders of His day was concerning their improper relationship and misinterpretation of the Law. The miss-guided leadership in Israel sought to motivate the people to keep the Law by increasing external restrictions on behavior and emphasizing the external penalties. Jesus corrected their abusive restrictions and illuminated the true intention of the Law as it related to a man's heart. He explained the right way to keep the Sabbath, treat your fellowman, etc. **He never abolished the principles within the Law; He defined them correctly as the scripture intended.** While *Deuteronomy 13* said that Jesus could not contradict the Law, *Deuteronomy 18* promised another Prophet like Moses who would have God's Word in His mouth. Jesus was that Prophet and if a person did not accept His direction about the Law, God said, *"I myself will call him into account"*. Jesus used divine authority to properly interpret Israel's Law; and now, His Holy Spirit is doing the same thing in us! I encourage you to spend some time examining the encounters that Jesus had with the religious leaders of His day to see if Jesus annulled the Law or taught them it's true intention. I have found that most of Jesus' statements <u>took the Law which was right and expounded upon **its righteous intentions.**</u> In this way, He was showing the right way to "Halakah" or walk out the Law.

With the theological foundation laid in the Older Testament in mind, look at the following quotations from the Newer Testament:

2 Tim 3:14-17
14 But as for you, **continue in what you have learned** and have become convinced of, because you know those from whom you learned it, 15 and how **from infancy you have known the Holy Scriptures,** which <u>are able to make you wise for salvation through faith in Christ Jesus</u>. 16 **All Scripture is God-breathed and is useful** for **teaching**, **rebuking**, **correcting** and **training in righteousness**, 17 so that the man of God may be thoroughly equipped for every good work.

In the past when I read this scripture, I thought the Newer Testament was in view. The words *"All Scripture"* can't refer to the Newer Testament alone (if at all) since the Newer Testament wasn't codified until 140 years after this was written. Indeed, the *"holy Scriptures"* referenced in verse **15** can only refer to the Tanakh. What Paul told Timothy is in perfect agreement with what the Older Testament says about the Law: "*…it is useful for* **teaching, rebuking, correcting,** *and* **training in righteousness**…" This is, yet one more, display of Paul's love for and understanding of the multifaceted Law. His theological foundation was rooted in the Law and he and the other Apostles saw it as useful for *"training in righteousness"* as well as the much emphasized *"correcting"*. Where has this been in our teaching? If we have only seen the Law as oppressive and hostile to us then we have been in error. If you look closely, you will see the theological foundation from the Law used frequently in all of the Apostles' writings.

1 John 5:1-4
5:1 Everyone who believes that Jesus is the Christ is born of God, and everyone who loves the father loves his child as well. 2 This is how we know that we love the children of God: by loving God and **carrying out his commands.** 3 **This is love for God: to obey his commands**. And **his commands are not burdensome**, 4 for everyone born of God overcomes the world.

Similarly to 2 Timothy, I used to mistakenly view this scripture only in the "light" of Newer Testament commands. That is however, not what the readers would have had in mind. The word for "*commands*" in this text is the Greek word "entolas". The corresponding word in Hebrew would be "mitzvah" which refers to the commands in the Law. Linguistic arguments aside, John's theological foundation was the Torah which said virtually the same thing as what the above scripture says. Compare *1 John 5:3* with ***Duet 13:3-4***, "*The LORD your God is testing **you to find out whether*** *you love him* *with all your heart and with all your soul. 4 It is the LORD your God you must follow, and him you must revere.* ***Keep his commands and obey him; serve him and hold fast to him.****"* Additionally, ***Psalm 1:1-3*** says the Law is a source of peace and a delight in keeping with John's phrase, "*...his commands are not burdensome*". In this way the entire Newer Testament is found within the Older Testament, you just have to look! Jeremiah said that God would take the Law (foundation for the Older Covenant) and put it on the heart. In principle, the change is the way we relate to the commands; however, the commands have not been abolished. **<u>Our motivation has become internal rather than external</u>**. The problem was that we were **unspiritual** while **the Law was spiritual (*Rom 7:14*)**...God gave us the Spirit of Jesus, the Holy Spirit to solve the problems of motivation and interpretation (***Ezek 36:27 & John 14:26***).

At this point it is probably necessary that I affirm my belief that I stand as righteous before God by way of Faith in Jesus alone. This righteousness is not by works, it is an act of Grace so that there is no room for boasting. (Eph 2:8***) Please don't misunderstand me! I am not advocating anything other than a proper view of the Law as useful for training in righteousness.

Spiritually Discerned

How do we, as believers, interpret Newer Testament commands? Think about the following passages:

- **1 Tim 2:9-10** I also want women to dress modestly, with decency and propriety, not with braided hair or gold or pearls or expensive clothes, 10 but with good deeds, appropriate for women who profess to worship God.
- **1 Cor 11:5-6** And every woman who prays or prophesies with her head uncovered dishonors her head — it is just as though her head were shaved . 6 If a woman does not cover her head, she should have her hair cut off; and if it is a disgrace for a woman to have her hair cut or shaved off, she should cover her head.
- **Romans 16:16, 1 Cor 16:20, 2 Cor 13:12, 1 Thess 5:26** All these passages contain imperative statements telling us to *"Greet one another with a holy kiss.."*

Don't we take into consideration the audience? Are their cultural norms important to understanding the scriptural instruction? Is understanding the problem within the local audience pertinent to understanding the direction being given in the letter? Ultimately, don't you have to rely on the Holy Spirit to teach, guide, direct, turn you towards His intentions for you regarding these scriptures? I could list many more scriptures in this vein, but the reality is that Christians rely on the Holy Spirit everyday to show them the proper way to relate to God's instructions. **Christians in Victorian era England may have potentially related differently to a scripture dealing with modesty than Christians in present day Amsterdam.** I am not advocating judging an individual's relationship with God by any external method. I am instead arguing that God has provided, by way of His written Word (including the Law), a means for an individual to confirm/weigh the leading of the Spirit. The Word and the Spirit are far from mutually exclusive; in fact, they must work in conjunction with each other for the Word to be "living" in the daily life of believers! Many times the Christian "catch all" used to render the Law useless is that we simply are "led by the Spirit". What then is the purpose of the Word? Why even posses a Bible? Certainly, the Holy Spirit can minister to someone without the written Word; but, does that mean that you should intentionally "handicap" yourself? Isn't that an insult to the blood of the martyrs who labored to get you the Bible? Was Timothy less "Spirit-led" because he knew the Law from adolescence? A thousand times NO! Paul said that the Law made Timothy *"wise for salvation"*. Certainly, there is a proper balance to being led by the counsel of the Spirit and the Word. One of the more difficult concepts that arises as we bring into view the importance of the Law is: how do Gentiles relate to the Law and is that different for Jews? I wish there were an easy answer! There is only one way to be saved (***Acts 4:12***). There is only one body of Christ (***Eph 4:4***). Jews and Gentiles are spiritually equal in Christ (***Gal 3:26-27***). Since salvation and equality are not in question between Jewish and Gentile believers anymore than they are between males and females, we should move on to function and calling. I have been tempted to believe that only Israelis had a relationship to the Law. That misunderstanding was based on pronoun usage in the Pauline epistles and on this Psalm:

Ps 147:19-20
19 He has revealed his word to Jacob,
His laws and decrees to Israel.

20 **He has done this for no other nation**;
they do not know his laws.

My idea was that Israel was the only one given the Law; and therefore, the only one instructed by it and the only one liberated from its curses penalties. As I have re-examined this principle I found enlightening scriptures.

Deut 4:5-8
5 See, I have taught you decrees and laws as the LORD my God commanded me, so that you may follow them in the land you are entering to take possession of it. 6 Observe them carefully, **for this will show your wisdom and understanding to the nations** , who will hear about all these decrees and say, "Surely this great nation is a wise and understanding people." 7 What other nation is so great as to have their gods near them the way the LORD our God is near us whenever we pray to him? 8 And what other nation is so great as **to have such righteous decrees and laws as this body of laws** I am setting before you today?

Ps 67:1-2
May God be gracious to us and bless us
and make his face shine upon us,
Selah
2 that **your ways may be known on earth**,
your salvation among all nations

These scriptures indicate that the Law given to Israel was intended to display the righteous character of God to the nations. Israel was to be an example for the nations. Even the nations without the Law were guilty and reproved for transgressing the principles within the Law.

Lev 18:23-24
23 "'Do not have sexual relations with an animal and defile yourself with it. A woman must not present herself to an animal to have sexual relations with it; that is a perversion.
24 "'Do not defile yourselves in any of these ways, because this is how the nations that I am going to drive out before **you became defiled**.

Lev 20:23
23 You must not live according to the customs of the nations I am going to drive out before you. **Because they did all these things, I abhorred them**.

It seems evident that even the Gentile nations had *some* relationship to the Law. In fact, the principles within the Law have been in existence since the creation. All mankind was under the "law of sin and death" that resulted from partaking in the "knowledge of good and evil". Tithing, sacrifice, circumcision and many other concepts expounded upon in the Law were present prior to the Law. Israel was the only nation ever given these righteous imperatives as a civil constitution for their nation. So while Gentiles may have a relationship to the righteous intentions of the Law, an Israeli may feel a greater obligation. **Righteous standards are righteous whether you are Mongolian or Israeli but the patriotic-nationalistic desire and calling to identify with Israel may be different.** Many men have set out to divide the Mosaic Law into categories (moral, civil, and ceremonial) and have used those categories to determine the relevance of the Law differently for Jews and Gentiles. While I agree that the Law may have differing significance for Jewish and Gentiles believers, I view the process of delineation as the role of the Holy Spirit and not work entrusted to any man. **I want to be clear**: I do not think any man has the right to tell a

Jew that he is/or is not obligated to anything in the Law; likewise, I do not think any man has the right to tell a Gentile that he should/or shouldn't do something contained within the Law. First of all in Christ, all penalties have been removed and the motivation is inward rather than external. Secondly, matters of cultural identity and customs should be decided by individuals as they are led by the Spirit and assisted by their Pastors. If an Ethiopian became a Christian, would you require him to dress in western cloths, eat western food, and attend church in a western style building? Unquestionably, the Gospel is not an American invention. If we would not require an Ethiopian Christian to lay aside his culture to come into Jesus, why would we even consider asking a Jewish person to give up his cultural identity (prescribed by God) to come into Jesus? As a matter of principle, it is reasonable to assume that someone with a very strong Jewish background may posses a calling by the Spirit to strongly identify with nationalistic aspects of the Law that a Gentile may not feel led to identify with. These cultural differences in function have always existed and have absolutely nothing to do with salvation. (Acts 15 addresses this issue as it relates to Jews making requirements of Gentiles…Oddly we now have the "shoe on the other foot") In my view this is no different than the variations in interpretation of the verses I started this section with that relate to cultural norms, relative modesty, and gender sensitivities. Furthermore, reasonable men who are generally "led by the Spirit" can come to different conclusions based on their individual calling and practice. **Romans 14:4** *"Who are you to judge someone else's servant? To his own master he stands or falls. And he will stand, for the Lord is able to make him stand."* Some Christians enjoy alcohol with out drunkenness and other Christians' convictions or circumstances will not allow them to do this. Certainly, the Kingdom is bigger than food and drink; Christians who drink wine can demonstrate in the Word that it is a liberty while Christians who do not can demonstrate in the Word why they shouldn't and the Spirit is potentially leading them both! These differences are spiritually discerned and largely dependent on circumstances, calling, and function in the body. In the same way, Jewish believers and Gentile believers may relate differently to the Law because of calling and function, and yet, be equals in Christ. A careful reading of *Acts 15* will reveal that the apostles laid no burden upon Gentile believers but also made no prohibition against the customs of Moses for Jewish believers. Instead, they gave instructions to both groups that would promote table fellowship as sign of equality. I believe this approach is more "Spirit Led" than the approach that simply throws away 1600 years of Divine revelation under the banner of being "led by the Spirit" alone. The latter approach is inconsistent with the purpose of the Holy Spirit and the scriptures themselves. I have chosen to be led by the Spirit of God and the counsel of the whole Word of God. I wonder if there would be less chaos in the "Charismatic Zoo" if the attitude of "No rules…Just right" wasn't so prevalent. When I say "rules" I am not speaking of punishment; I am speaking of righteous standards that provide direction in the leading of the Spirit. When used properly the Law shows the Christian the good he is free to do and warns him about the trappings of sin! Titus and Timothy were both Spirit-filled believers who elected to take different stances on circumcision because of their cultural identities, calling, and function within the body. I am convinced both were *free* to take their respective stances. (***Gal 2:3 and Acts 16:3***) A proper view of the Law promotes this freedom.

Peter Said It Was Difficult

I remarked earlier that I took some comfort from the fact that even Peter considered the Pauline epistles difficult. This should not be misconstrued to mean that they are not beneficial. Every believer that has truly engaged the sacred text has come away with a profound appreciation for the "Apostle to the Gentiles". He is a champion of the Faith that is to be admired and imitated. As the nature of Paul's true relationship to the Law began to become clearer to me, I couldn't help but marvel at the wisdom of God. Since Paul remained a Pharisee and a faithful observer of the Torah, he was uniquely qualified among the apostles to carry out the task of correcting those who maligned the true purpose of the Torah. Paul was formally educated in the strictest Pharisaic order and his credentials exceeded those of the other apostles and were beyond reproach by the common person; so if he made strong statements concerning the misuse of the Torah, his critics would find it hard to question his love for the Torah. If Oliver North (who served in the Marines for 22 years and was awarded the Silver Star, the Bronze Star, and two Purple Hearts) makes a statement critical of this country, only foolish people would question his patriotism. Likewise, Paul was an Israeli patriot and only those who greatly misunderstood his "*difficult*" writings questioned his love for the Torah. As we begin examining the Pauline epistles, please allow me a liberal measure of grace. I have not set out to write a commentary or even a book. <u>My hope has been to promote a balanced view of the Torah that acknowledges its relevance, benefits, and limitations</u>. I am a preacher and, as you undoubtedly are now aware, I lack the aptitude for written communication. Your patience and mercy are greatly appreciated. Previously we covered the following sections:

- **Baby with the Bath water** (The Law should not be thrown out with the "curses of the Law")
- **Clear Historical Record** (The early Church and particularly Paul was undeniably Torah-observant)
- **A Theological Foundation** (The God-given theological foundation for all revelation is the Torah. The Jewish Apostles relied on this foundation ardently)
- **Dispensational Segmentation or "Unbroken" Promises** (It is unscriptural to divide the scripture into segments that no longer apply)
- **Internal and External Motivation** (The major improvements in the Newer Covenant are that believers would be cleansed "made righteous" and have the Law impressed on them by way of the indwelling & empowering Holy Spirit)
- **Spiritually Discerned** (The indwelling of the Holy Spirit and the counsel of the Word of God are the means by which we interpret our individual relationship to the Law that is written both in the Holy Scriptures and upon our hearts)

My strategy in discussing each of the previous sections was to open BIG. Much in the same way a heavy-weight boxer hopes for an early knock out in a boxing match. If you are totally un-persuaded at this point then there is little hope for a decision at the end of the round. While I intend to cover some of the "difficult" writings, my purpose is not to write a commentary. Examining the previous sections should have begun the process of opening your eyes to the *"wonderful things"* in the Law so that you will be able to properly discern Paul's intentions in his writing. The major error that we suffer from is interpreting the Law in the "light" of the statements in the Pauline epistles instead of interpreting the statements in the Pauline epistles in the "light" of the Law. We have the funnel upside down and therefore have a narrow view of the Law. I have set my sights on turning the funnel right side up! When viewing the Pauline epistles, you must take into account the broader volume of scripture. Without laying the foundation again, let me list some of the noteworthy points I have argued for up to this point:

- Peter, Paul, James, Ananias, the Jerusalem Elders, and the community of believers in Jerusalem were all living in obedience to the Law.
- Paul considered himself a Pharisee nearly 30 years after the cross.
- Paul and his traveling companions were accepted among Jews in the synagogues on the Sabbath, testifying to Paul's obedience to the Law.
- Paul taught effectively about Jesus using the Law of Moses.
- The Law was the original measuring stick for all successive revelation.
- The scripture says the Law is a delight, something to be meditated on, perfect, reviving the soul, altogether righteous, a joy to the heart, more precious than gold, and sweeter than honey.
- The Law is a source of hope and freedom reviving the soul, making wise the simple, giving joy to the heart, and giving light to the eyes.
- Jeremiah's description of a Newer Covenant was taking the Older Covenant Law and impressing it on the heart and mind of Israel.
- Ezekiel's description of the Newer Covenant was cleansing Israel and then

- giving them the Holy Spirit to move them to keep the Law.
- Jesus can be directly quoted as saying, *"I have not come to abolish them* (the laws) *but to fulfill them...not the least stroke of a pen, will by any means disappear from the Law...whoever practices and teaches these commands will be called great in the kingdom of heaven"*
- The bulk of Jesus teaching illuminated the proper way to keep and relate to the Law.
- There is an undeniable continuity between the precepts of the Tanakh and the Newer Testament as demonstrated by the relationship between (***1 John 5***) and (***Deuteronomy 13:1-3, Psalm 1:1-3***) as well as (***2 Timothy 3:16***) and the Psalms.
- The Apostles ardently opposed forcing Gentiles to keep Jewish customs; but, Jewish believers were never told to give up their cultural identity derived from the Law.
- The goal of Peter's vision and the later Jerusalem Council was to encourage table fellowship as a sign of equality in the body of Christ.
- The Holy Spirit works in conjunction with God's Holy Word to lead a person.

Now let us consider some of Paul's statements. Paul frequently quoted the Law as authoritative even when the audience was predominantly Gentile believers.

Eph 6:1-3
6:1 Children, obey your parents in the Lord, for this is right. 2 "Honor your father and mother"-which is the first commandment with a promise— 3 "that it may go well with you and that you may enjoy long life on the earth."

Paul quotes **Deuteronomy 5:16** to the Ephesian Church as something that is "*right*" even in the Newer Testament era. I believe this is because what was righteous in 1600 BC <u>was still righteous around 60 AD</u>. However, Paul did not mention any penalty associated with the "mitzvah" to honor your parents although **Deuteronomy 21:18** lists such a penalty. Paul does, on the other hand, list the promise associated with the command "*that it may go well with you and that you may enjoy long life on the earth*". This is consistent with the concept that Jesus took upon himself all the "*curse of the law*" (***Gal 3:13***) while leaving us as heirs and co-heirs of the "*promises*" **(Eph 3:6)**. In examining what my relationship is to the Law as a Gentile, I have wondered what I will teach my children regarding their relationship to the Law. At the moment, I can see myself in the future discussing this "mitzvah" with my son Judah. The hypothetical conversation, as I envision it, would go something like this:

Judah, your teacher called today and said that you were disrespectful for the 3rd time this week. Son, you simply must correct this behavior. Children in ancient Israel who persisted in insolent behavior, to the point that they were considered incorrigible, were punished by stoning them. Truthfully, that is what your sin deserves; but, you can praise Jesus who took that punishment upon himself in your place! He was never disrespectful or disobedient; and yet, He was put to death as a law breaker in your place. In this way he protected you from falling under a curse; but, He also preserved a promise for you. The scripture also says that children who obey their parents will have successful long lives! Let's pray and thank Jesus for taking all of the cursing that you deserve while leaving you all the blessings. Let's ask Him to empower you with His Holy Spirit to live in a respectful and obedient manner, as He did, so that you will have a long and successful life.

I am confident that anyone with children will see the wisdom in this. Can you imagine telling a 9 year old...Just be led by the Spirit, with no additional guidance. The idea is absurd! Additionally, it is equally absurd to say that a maturing Christian no longer needs any counsel from the Torah because he is now Spirit-led. Why, then, did Paul quote the Torah to Spirit-filled Gentiles? So then, we see Paul using the Law as applicable to even the Ephesian Church. Look at this one:

1 Cor 9:3-11
3 This is my defense to those who sit in judgment on me. 4 Don't we have the right to food and drink? 5 Don't we have the right to take a believing wife along with us, as do the other apostles and the Lord's brothers and Cephas? 6 Or is it only I and Barnabas who must work for a living?

7 Who serves as a soldier at his own expense? Who plants a vineyard and does not eat of its grapes? Who tends a flock and does not drink of the milk? 8 <u>**Do I say this merely from a human point of view**</u>**? Doesn't the Law say the same thing**? 9 **For it is written in the Law of Moses:** "Do not muzzle an ox while it is treading out the grain." Is it about oxen that God is concerned? 10 <u>Surely he says this for us, doesn't he</u>? ***Yes, this was written for us***, because when the plowman plows and the thresher threshes, they ought to do so in the hope of sharing in the harvest. 11 If we have sown spiritual seed among you, is it too much if we reap a material harvest from you?

52

How many Pastors would be happy if we rendered this one inoperative? Paul's basis for his right to financial support is the Law. The words *"Do I say this from a human point of view? Doesn't the Law say the same thing? For it is written in the Law of Moses...Yes, this was written for us..."* are difficult to argue away. Paul clearly saw the Law's righteous intentions as applicable for today! The words *"Doesn't the Law say the same thing?"* indicate that Paul expected them to have knowledge of the Law (even though they were Spirit-led...I say this sarcastically). How many Christians today would be familiar with this quote from ***Deuteronomy 25:4*** if Paul did not refer to it in both 1 Corinthians and 1 Timothy? I suspect that not many would know of its existence. Rather, than continuing to point out the hundreds of allusions to and quotations from the Law found in the Pauline epistles, we will move on to the "problem" scriptures.

Galatians

When reading the letter to the Galatians (Galatians means "land of the Celts") it is important to consider the audience. Paul is primarily addressing Gentile believers. Among the scriptures that allow you to positively identify the audience are:

- **Galatians 3:1**, *"You foolish Galatians!"* The book of James is addressed to the twelve tribes scattered, the book of Romans is addressed to those in Rome, the book of Jude is addressed to those loved by God, and the book of Galatians seems to be addressed to those who called themselves Galatians. It is unlikely that a Jew would do this even if he lived in Galatia.
- **Galatians 4:8**, *"Formerly, when you did not know God, you were slaves to those who by*

nature are not gods." This verse does not indicate a past in Judaism; it indicates a past in Gentile paganism.
- **Galatians 5:2**, *"Mark my words! I, Paul, tell you that if you let yourselves be circumcised, Christ will be of no value to you at all"*. This would hardly make sense if the audience was Jewish. All Jews were circumcised on the 8th day of their lives. Paul has to be addressing a Gentile audience.
- **Galatians 6:12**, *"Those who want to make a good impression outwardly are trying to compel you to be circumcised."* Again, it is not possible to relate this scripture to those born as Jews. The audience must be of Gentile origin.

Now that you know the audience is Gentile believers, it is important for you to discern the reason for the letter. The Galatian letter was written to address specific problems. We need to know what they were in order to provide the context for Paul's corrections.

- **Galatians 1:6**, *"I am astonished that you are so quickly deserting the one who called you by the grace of Christ and are turning to a different gospel—which is really no gospel at all. Evidently some people are throwing you into confusion and are trying to pervert the gospel of Christ."* This verse indicates that the Galatians were being tempted by a perversion of the gospel.
- **Galatians 3:3**, *"After beginning in the Spirit, are you now trying to attain your goal by human effort?"* The perverted gospel that they were being tempted by was based on human effort.

- **Galatians 5:12 & 6:12,** *"As for those agitators, I wish they would go the whole way and emasculate themselves"* and *"Those who want to make a good impression outwardly are trying to compel you to be circumcised"* The agitators were Judaizers.

The context for the letter to the Galatians is that Gentile believers (formerly pagans) were being thrown into confusion by Jews who misunderstood the Torah and were in error. Their specific errors all related to a legalistic perversion of the Law into a means for salvation and acceptance. They tried to require Gentile believers to be circumcised and keep all of the customs of Moses before they would consider the Gentiles saved or grant them the acceptance of fellowship. These errors contradict the Torah itself and the directives given to Gentile believers in *Acts 15*. As we examine the verses to follow, it is imperative that you keep both the problem being addressed and Paul's self identification as a Pharisee and observer of the Law in mind. The following verses are often distorted to mean that the Law is only negative and has no place among Christians. **The historical practices of the Apostles conclusively negate this view**, but let's examine the verses anyway.

Galatians 3:10-14
10 All who rely on observing the law are under a curse, for it is written: "Cursed is everyone who does not continue to do everything written in the Book of the Law." 11 Clearly no one is justified before God by the law, because, "The righteous will live by faith." 12 The law is not based on faith; on the contrary, "The man who does these things will live by them." 13 Christ redeemed us from the curse of the law by becoming a curse for us, for it is written: "Cursed is everyone who is hung on a tree." 14 He redeemed us in order that the blessing given

to Abraham might come to the Gentiles through Christ Jesus, so that by faith we might receive the promise of the Spirit.

In verses **10 & 11**, we find Paul using the truth of the Torah to correct the false assertions of the Judaizers. The Judaizers saw observance of the Law as a means of salvation, rather than, a right way to live that promoted trust in God for salvation. Salvation could never be obtained by legalistic observance of the Law since no human being could perform the Law without failing. At the same time the Law taught the righteous standards of God, it also pointed out sin in sinful man. <u>Paul is teaching the Gentile believers the futility of legalistic self-righteousness.</u> Remember the Torah never taught salvation as keeping the commands. Salvation has always been by trusting in God (**Psalm 22:4-5**), but those who trusted and loved God also kept his commands (***Duet 13:3-4 & 1 John 5:3***). Judaizers got this relationship backwards. They saw keeping the commands as salvation. This is very similar to the present day debate over faith and works. While you cannot work your way into salvation, those who are saved certainly have works. Depending on the audience in view you may emphasize the need for works accompanying salvation (perhaps to a Baptist person) or you may down play works focusing on sincere faith (perhaps to a Catholic person). Paul ends verse **11** by quoting the Tanakh, *"...the righteous will live by faith."* This was not a new concept! The only method of salvation that there has ever been was to trust God and be credited with righteousness. Paul, who himself was a Pharisee and a Law-observant Jewish believer, was supremely qualified to correct the Judaizer's legalistic perversion of the Torah without being misunderstood as being anti-Law. Let's move on to verse **12**.

12 The law is not based on faith; on the contrary, "The man who does these things will live by them."

The reason I have gone through such pains to point out the audience and the problem is to provide a means of understanding the idea being addressed in this verse **12**. You simply can't reconcile the overall witness of the Scriptures with this statement by a superficial reading. The clear historical practice of the Apostles, the Tanakh, and Paul's own statements confirm that the Law was good, spiritual, holy, and righteous. This scripture is only misunderstood if the context is ignored. The **implied** meaning is that the way the Judaizers were approaching the Law was not based on faith. Their legalistic approach totally displaced faith. They had, through external legalistic regulations, destroyed the intent of the very Law that they claimed to uphold by approaching it incorrectly. *Isaiah 1:10-19* addressed this legalistic misapplication of the Torah and pointed to the true intentions of the Law that were to be written on the hearts of believers.

Isa 1:10-19
0 Hear the word of the LORD, you rulers of Sodom; **listen to the law of our God**, you people of Gomorrah! 11 "The multitude of your sacrifices — what are they to me?" says the LORD."I have more than enough of burnt offerings, of rams and the fat of fattened animals; I have no pleasure in the blood of bulls and lambs and goats. 12 When you come to appear before me, who has asked this of you, this trampling of my courts? 13 **Stop bringing meaningless offerings**! <u>Your incense is detestable to me</u>. New Moons, Sabbaths and convocations — I cannot bear your **evil** assemblies. 14 Your New Moon festivals and your appointed feasts <u>my soul hates</u>. They have become a burden to me; I am weary of bearing them. 15 When you spread out

your hands in prayer, I will hide my eyes from you; even if you offer many prayers, I will not listen. Your hands are full of blood; 16 **wash and make yourselves clean**. Take your evil deeds out of my sight! Stop doing wrong, 17 **learn to do right! Seek justice, encourage the oppressed. Defend the cause of the fatherless, plead the case of the widow.**
18 "Come now, let us reason together, "says the LORD. "Though your sins are like scarlet, they shall be as white as snow; though they are red as crimson, they shall be like wool. 19 <u>If you are willing and obedient</u>, you will eat the best from the land;

You can see from this quotation in Isaiah that God was not pleased by "rote", mechanical observance alone. The Law was intended to teach the people to care about what God cared about: justice, the oppressed, the fatherless, and the widow. Additionally, the Law was supposed to show the world their failings; starting with Israel. In this way the Law taught righteousness and displayed the need for salvation. Considering the audience and the problem they were facing, you can discern the intended meaning of Paul's words in verses **10, 11,** and **12. He was teaching against reliance on the Law for salvation and condemned the false method advocated by the Judaizers as contrary to the way of faith**. Let's look at the final verses in the passage (**13 & 14**).

13 Christ redeemed us from the curse of the law by becoming a curse for us, for it is written: "Cursed is everyone who is hung on a tree." 14 He redeemed us in order that the blessing given to Abraham might come to the Gentiles through Christ Jesus, so that by faith we might receive the promise of the Spirit.

In teaching against the reliance on the Law for salvation (which was never its purpose), Paul pointed out the *"curse of the law"* which falls on everyone who fails to keep all of the Law. In other words, all Israel was under the curses prescribed in the Law because of human weakness and failure to keep the Law. Verse **13** is instruction on how Israel could be/would be saved from the cursing. Jesus took the curse for Israel. Verse **14** tells the Galatians how the solution to cursing, be it the Mosaic penalties or the law of sin and death, can be applied to them through the faith of Abraham. In putting it all together, I would like to quote from the Complete Jewish Bible: (the formatting is unaltered, the bolded, italicized, and bracketed words appear in the translation)

Galatians 3:10-14
10 For everyone who depends on legalistic observance of *Torah* commands lives under a curse, since it is written, **"Cursed is everyone who does not keep on doing everything written in the Scroll of the *Torah*."** 11 Now it is evident that no one comes to be declared righteous by God through legalism, since **"The person who is righteous will attain life by trusting and being faithful."** 12 Furthermore, legalism is not based on trusting and being faithful, but on [a misuse of] the text that says, **"Anyone who does these things will attain life through them."** 13 The Messiah redeemed us from the curse pronounced in the *Torah* by becoming cursed on our behalf; for the *Tanakh* says, **"Everyone who hangs from a stake comes under a curse."** 14 Yeshua

the Messiah did this so that in
union with him the Gentiles might
receive the blessing announced to
Avraham, so that through trusting
and being faithful, we might
receive what was promised, namely,
the Spirit.

The verdict is that Paul was addressing a legalistic perversion of the Torah into something it was never designed to be! He was teaching the Galatians that faith is the only means of salvation. Do you remember the example earlier of Oliver North? Would you interpret a couple of statements by Oliver North to mean that he was anti-American without considering his 22 years of patriotic service? Paul was a Pharisee who took deliberate steps to prove that he was not teaching against the customs of Moses. The book of Acts clearly demonstrates this fact (***Acts 21:24***). No doubt a superficial reading of this passage could be confusing, even Peter said "*His letters contain some things that are <u>hard to understand</u>, which ignorant and unstable people distort, as they do the other Scriptures, to their own destruction. Therefore, dear friends, since you already know this, be on your guard so that you may not be carried away by <u>the error of lawless men</u>*". I urge you to take the time to prayerfully consider the context in which Paul wrote his letter. The conclusion you will come to is that Paul was never anti-Law; but, he was ardently against a legalistic misuse of the Law that sought to place Gentiles under the penalty of the Law. The next passage that is typically used to render the Law as inapplicable today is:

Gal 3:23-25
23 Before this faith came, we were held prisoners by the law, locked up until faith should be revealed. 24 So the law was put in charge to lead us to Christ

that we might be justified by faith. 25 Now that faith has come, we are no longer under the supervision of the law.

I feel very fortunate to have sat under excellent teaching regarding the Greek words in this text. The Law in this passage is likened to a Greek word "Paidagogos". What is usually taught about the Greek concept of a "Paidagogos" is that the term refers to a custodian or schoolmaster. Modern translations have opted for phrases other than "schoolmaster" because the Greek concept of "Paidagogos" had no teaching functions and refers mostly to a disciplinarian figure. If our explanation stops here with a superficial reading, you would come away with the idea that the Law was simply a dispensational-temporary custodian destined to pass away with the arrival of faith. This is, in fact, how I understood the verses for years. Before explaining the meaning of the verses, I want to remind you that the theological foundation of the Apostles said that the Law was: a delight, something to be meditated on, perfect, reviving the soul, altogether righteous, a joy to the heart, more precious than gold, sweeter than honey, a source of hope, freedom, reviving the soul, making wise the simple, giving joy to the heart, and giving light to the eyes. Now let's read the passage in the New Revised Standard Version translation.

Gal 3:23-25
23 Now before faith came, we were imprisoned and guarded under the law until faith would be revealed. 24 Therefore the law was our disciplinarian until Christ came, so that we might be justified by faith. 25 But now that faith has come, we are no longer subject to a disciplinarian,

I have been taught that the Law was related to the "Paidagogos" because the Law was not meant to teach; it was only meant to restrain and point out sin. This teaching is partially correct and was a noteworthy revelation, but it is incomplete! One of the many functions of the Law was a disciplinarian or "Paidagogos"; but, this was certainly not the only function! This analogy was used to specifically counter act legalism that sought to nullify Christ's redeeming us from the *"curse of the Law"* by placing us back under the *'curse of the Law"* or its penalties. This analogy was not intended to represent Paul's comprehensive view of the Law. Nor was it intended to be a perfect analogy for all situations; anymore than, Jesus' analogy of himself as a door. Analogies are by nature imperfect and only used to convey a point. If punishment without teaching were the only purpose of the Law then you would have to eliminate the Psalms as being uninspired and reckon Paul as a hypocrite for his own relationship to the Law (I would quote all the supporting verses again but I am scared that the redundancy would be offensive). Israel was under the disciplinarian (*curses of the Law*); until as both Jeremiah and Ezekiel foresaw, God would give them His Holy Spirit so that they would be internally motivated rather than externally motivated to keep the Law. The Holy Spirit would move them to keep the Law rather than the penalties (which are removed in Christ) being the motivator. The Judaizers were trying to undo the salvation of the Gentiles by placing them under the disciplinary aspects of the Law that no one could be justified by…not even Israel. The new relationship to the Law was not based on its disciplinarian supervision; it is based on loving and trusting God and wanting to do what is right. This is very much like an adolescent who lives a relatively wholesome life because his parents punish him if he doesn't; but, the day comes when he becomes an adult and will have to live those same righteous principles without fear of punishment. His maturing does not eliminate the right things his parents taught him; the maturing changes his relationship to them. He is expected to *trust* the way his parents said was right and to walk in it out of love even if they don't punish him anymore. Why did Paul write this to the Galatians? They were being persuaded to come under the penalty of the Law by viewing it as a means of salvation. This inappropriate and futile legalistic method was advocated by Judaizers, who perverted the Law into a fearful taskmaster, as a mean forcing the Galatians into a perversion of Judaism as a requirement for salvation and acceptance. Since this Judaizing effort was contrary to ***Acts 15*** and the true intent of the Law, Paul strongly opposed it. Paul's own words confirm that faith does not stand in opposition to the Law used properly: *"Do we, then, nullify the law by this faith? Not at all! Rather, we uphold the law."* Putting ***Galatians 3:10-14*** and ***3:23-25*** together looks like this: (I am purposely quoting from two translations)

Galatians 3:10-14 (The Complete Jewish Bible)
10 For everyone who depends on legalistic observance of *Torah* commands lives under a curse, since it is written, **"Cursed is everyone who does not keep on doing everything written in the Scroll of the *Torah*."** 11 Now it is evident that no one comes to be declared righteous by God through legalism, since **"The person who is righteous will attain life by trusting and being faithful."** 12 Furthermore, legalism is not based on trusting and being faithful, but on [a misuse of] the text that says, **"Anyone who does these things will attain life through them."** 13 The Messiah redeemed us from the curse pronounced in the

Torah by becoming cursed on our behalf; for the *Tanakh* says, **"Everyone who hangs from a stake comes under a curse."** 14 Yeshua the Messiah did this so that in union with him the Gentiles might receive the blessing announced to Avraham, so that through trusting and being faithful, we might receive what was promised, namely, the Spirit.

Gal 3:23-25 (the New Revised Standard Version) 23 Now before faith came, we were imprisoned and guarded under the law until faith would be revealed. 24 Therefore the law was our disciplinarian until Christ came, so that we might be justified by faith. 25 But now that faith has come, we are no longer subject to a disciplinarian,

Paraphrasing verses **23-25** would sound like this: Before we (Jews as a nation) were able to fully trust God, our nation was restrained by the disciplinary aspects of the law until a better relationship of faith would be revealed to the nation. In this way the disciplinarian aspects of the Law served the nation until Christ came, so that it would be evident to everyone that our justification would have to come by faith (not 'rote' obedience). Now that this full revelation of faith has come we are not to be restrained by the disciplinary aspects of the Law (we are free).

Paul's point in referring to Israel's liberation from the disciplinary aspects of the Law was: Israel didn't even relate to the Law through legalism for justification, but, was justified through faith in Jesus. If Israel wasn't justified through legalism then certainly Gentiles shouldn't fall subject to a misuse of the Law, but, should embrace faith as the true means of salvation! No doubt, some will feel like my paraphrasing is an abuse of the text and others will approve of it. The Complete Jewish Bible and the Amplified are very similar to my paraphrasing. I am not attempting to re-translate the passage; instead, I am just presenting my understanding of the passage. In every case throughout the letter to the Galatians, the true meaning of the passages is dependant on considering the entire context of the situation being addressed. Most of the common theology on this subject is thoroughly untenable when placed in the "light" of the Tanakh and the practice of the Apostles as contained in the book of Acts. It is not hard to see why Paul said the things he did when you understand the problems he was trying to correct. Whatever view you come to regarding the interpretation of the text, it must be consistent with the "unbroken" Cannon of Scripture, the practice of the Apostles, and the character of the author. For brevity's sake, I will refer to a couple more scriptures in Galatians; but, leave the interpretive work to you.

Gal 3:26-28
26 You are all sons of God through faith in Christ Jesus, 27 for all of you who were baptized into Christ have clothed yourselves with Christ. 28 There is neither Jew nor Greek, slave nor free, male nor female, for you are all one in Christ Jesus.

This scripture and its parallel passages in Ephesians and Colossians are sometimes argued to mean that the Jew has absolutely no distinctiveness left and the Mosaic Covenant is cancelled. Please, investigate this notion. I am persuaded that the verses speak about our equality in Christ and not a total unity in calling and function. Males and females are equal in Christ, and yet, quite different in function and calling. Likewise, the scripture is rife with functional differences between Jewish believers and Gentile believers (I leave the discovery of those verses to you…but they are everywhere).

Gal 4:8-11

8 Formerly, <u>when you did not know God</u>, you were slaves to those who by nature <u>are not gods</u>. 9 But now that you know God — or rather are known by God — how is it that you are turning back **to those weak and miserable principles**? Do you wish to be enslaved by them all over again? 10 You are observing special days and months and seasons and years! 11 I fear for you, that somehow I have wasted my efforts on you.

These verses are sometimes referenced in trying to make the point that the Law is totally inoperable. It saddens me to think that people would assume that Paul was referring to the Law. After reading all that is said in the Tanakh about the *"wonderful things"* in the Law, I hope you know that Paul would not refer to a correct use of the Law as *"weak and miserable principles"*. Furthermore, he would not refer to Passover, the Sabbath, or Pentecost as weak and miserable since he personally observed them. Please, examine the passage closely. I believe you will come to one of two conclusions: (First possibility) The Galatians were *"formerly"* pagans and in addition to their present susceptibility to legalism, they also were tempted to revert to Astrology or some other pagan practice. (Second possibility) The perversion of the Torah that the Galatians were being tempted to embrace was *"weak and miserable"* and the false approach to the Jewish feasts was a waste of time. I am convinced that the first option is the one that applies but I leave it to you to discern (Judaism doesn't designate special **months** and **seasons**…I know some scholars think this refers to the head of months and seasonal feasts, but I am un-persuaded).

Before moving on to other scriptures outside of Galatians, I thought it would be good to point out a previously held view that *Galatians 3:15-17* indicates is a hypocritical position. Though not often verbalized, I used to consider the Mosaic Covenant as a temporary "parenthetical" insertion that resulted from a lack of faith in Israel. Since in my former view it was temporary, based on a misreading of the epistles, I reasoned that it could now be totally disregarded. While in that vein of thought, look at Paul's words to the Galatians on a similar subject:

Gal 3:15-17
15 Brothers, let me take an example from everyday life. Just as no one can set aside or add to a human covenant that has been duly established, so it is in this case. 16 The promises were spoken to Abraham and to his seed. The Scripture does not say "and to seeds," meaning many people, but "and to your seed," meaning one person, who is Christ. 17 What I mean is this: **The law, introduced 430 years later, does not set aside the covenant previously established by God** and thus do away with the promise.

Granted, Paul is saying the Abrahamic Covenant wasn't set aside by the Mosaic (and we all agree with that), but isn't it hypocritical then to turn around and say the Mosaic is replaced by the Newer Covenant? Did any of the biblical covenants replace the others? In my view the Mosaic is not defunct and inoperative, we simply relate to it differently through Jesus than Israel did prior to Jesus. I am tempted to cover other scriptures in Galatians; but, I am positive that I have at least given you the opportunity to examine your view of the Law to determine if your view is as balanced as the view portrayed in the unified Word of God (Whole Bible).

Romans

I will not spend much time in Romans because the arguments are largely the same as we have seen in Galatians. Romans is one of my favorite books; and, the reshaping of my views on the Torah have only enhanced my love for this epistle. A dear friend and mentor in the Lord got a beautiful revelation into the context of the book of Romans. The insight related to both the audience and the problems being addressed in the book. I am eternally grateful for his revelation because it has made Romans infinitely easier to understand. The context is as follows: Paul is writing to a mixed congregation of both Jewish believers and Gentile believers. Two major problems existed in the congregation. The first was that Jewish believers with some "Judaizing" tendencies were considering themselves superior to the Gentiles. The second is that the Gentiles may have had a propensity to retaliate with boasting over their new found positions. The major emphasis of the corrections seems to address the first problem. Again, I can't help but marvel at the wisdom of God for using Paul to address this issue because of his superior qualifications and un-reproachable love for the Torah. As the "Apostle to the Gentiles" his words carried special weight to Gentile hearers and as a Pharisee his words carried special weight with his Jewish hearers. Chapters *1* and **2** largely identify the problems at hand and begin the process of correcting them by demonstrating that both Jews and Gentiles are under the power of sin. I can't help but pause at Chapter **3** to read the following words:

Rom 3:1-4
3:1 What advantage, then, is there in being a Jew, or what value is there in circumcision? 2 **Much in every way!** First of all, they have been **entrusted with the very words of God**. 3 What if some did not have faith? Will their lack of faith nullify God's faithfulness? 4 Not at all! Let God be true, and every man a liar.

It was an advantage in every way to be *"entrusted with the very words of God"*. What words of God were they entrusted with? Certainly, he is speaking of the Tanakh which includes the Law. Apparently, there were no silly notions that learning the Law was contrary to being led by the Spirit. In verse *21*, we find the first scripture I could think of that is commonly used to render the Law as unimportant.

Rom 3:21
21 But now a righteousness from God, apart from law, has been made known, to which the Law and the Prophets testify.

The basic line of reasoning, for those who misunderstand this verse, seems to be: Since righteousness comes by a way other than the Law, the Law is opposed to righteousness or at the very least is unimportant to righteousness. Nothing could be further from the truth! Salvation comes by trusting in the Lord. The first three chapters in Romans are put forth to prove that both Jews and Gentiles are under the power of sin. The Law is not opposed to righteousness; it demonstrates righteousness or the lack there of! In fact, in Israel's case, it thoroughly demonstrated the lack of righteousness; but, in Jesus' case it proved Him thoroughly righteous. No one can hope to be declared righteous by the Law; but, through identification with and trust in Jesus we can uphold the righteous standards of the Law. Paul refers to

Gentiles doing this in ***Rom 2:13-15***, "*For it is not those who hear the law who are righteous in God's sight, but <u>it is those who obey the law who will be declared righteous</u>. 14(Indeed, when Gentiles, who do not have the law, do by nature things required by the law, they are a law for themselves, even though they do not have the law, 15 since they show that <u>the requirements of the law are written on their hearts</u>, their consciences also bearing witness, and their thoughts now accusing, now even defending them.)*" Ironically, this very verse is also often used to say that we don't need the Law! The argument says that the requirements are written on our hearts and consequently there is no need to learn the Law. What foolishness! Why handicap yourself? As I said earlier, this is an insult to those martyred to get you the Bible. That is why Paul said it was an "*…advantage…in every way…*(to be a Jew since) they *have been entrusted with the very words of God*" The 3rd chapter closes with a summation, "*Do we, then nullify the law by this faith? Not at all! Rather, we uphold the law.*" Chapter 4 goes on to expound on, through Abraham's example, how those outside and inside of Israel are equally credited with righteousness by faith. Chapters **5** & **6** speak of the new peace we have in Christ since we are **dead to sin and alive in Him** (whether Jew or Gentile). The concept of being dead to sin and alive in Him is carried into the next chapter by way of an analogy. This brings us to the one most of you have been waiting for, ***Romans 7***.

Rom 7:1-4
7:1 Do you not know, brothers — for I am speaking to men who know the law — that the law has authority over a man only as long as he lives? 2 For example, by law a married woman is bound to her husband as long as he is alive, but if her husband dies, she is released from the law of marriage. 3 So then, if she marries another man while her husband

is still alive, she is called an adulteress. But if her husband dies, she is released from that law and is not an adulteress, even though she marries another man.

First, take note that he is addressing "*men who know the law*". Sadly that description isn't fitting for most 21st century Christians, although, it was true of nearly every 1st century Christian. Paul uses this analogy to relate our identification with the death of Jesus to dieing to the "*curses of the Law*". Why do I say that? When Jesus died as a law breaker in our place, He received all the penalties of the Law that a person could receive. He was put to death in our stead or in our place (just as if we literally died). Paul's point is that the penalty of being declared an adulteress is only valid if both parties to the covenant are alive! When one spouse dies, the other is released. In the same way, we who died to sin and the penalties of sin through Jesus are free to be "married" to the risen Christ. In verses **4**, I am going to insert wording to help you follow my point. (My insertions will be identified by both parentheses and underlining to help you delineate my comment from the actual text. They will only appear in verses **4-6**.)

4 So, my brothers, you also died to the law (<u>curses or penalty of the Law</u>) through the body of Christ, that you might belong to another, to him who was raised from the dead, in order that we might bear fruit to God.

Whether you agree with me or not, you must reconcile Paul's words with the Tanakh, Paul's lifestyle, and the practice of the Apostles. I have found what I believe is the "key" to reconciling all of these in a harmonious manner. This hermeneutic can be consistently applied to the epistles and does not feel "forced" to me. Look at verses **5-6**:

5 For when we were controlled by the sinful nature, the sinful passions aroused by the law were at work in our bodies, so that we bore fruit for death. 6 But now, by dying to what once bound us (<u>curses or penalty of the Law</u>), we have been released from the law (<u>curses or penalty of the Law</u>) so that we serve in the new way of the Spirit (<u>explained by Ezekiel as the Spirit moving you to keep the Law</u>), and not in the old way of the written code (<u>a system that punished you for not rightly performing the Law</u>).

I hope this is as enlightening to you as it is to me! We died to all the penalties of the Law by dieing with Christ. We are now set free from the *"curse of the Law"* to serve God by the Spirit's empowerment to rightly live the Law (***Ezek 36:27***). We are no longer subject to a code that condemns us by prescribing temporal penalties for sin; we are motivated internally by the Spirit to keep and properly interpret the Law that is written in the scrolls, on the mind, and in our hearts. This is the manner, in which, Jesus kept the Law; He was perfectly led by the Spirit and never broke a single Law.

Rom 7:7-12
7 What shall we say, then? **Is the law sin? Certainly not**! Indeed I would not have known what sin was except through the law. For I would not have known what coveting really was if the law had not said, "Do not covet." 8 **But sin**, seizing the opportunity afforded by the commandment, **produced in me every kind of covetous desire**. For apart from law, sin is dead. 9 Once I was alive apart from law; but when the commandment came, sin sprang to life and I died. 10 **I found that the very commandment that was intended to bring life actually brought death**. 11 **For sin**, seizing the opportunity afforded by the commandment,

deceived me, and through the commandment put me to death. 12 **So then, the law is holy, and the commandment is holy, righteous and good.**

Verses **7-12** seem so clear to me know! The Law is not and never has been bad. It is good, righteous, and holy. The problem was with the failings of human weakness and sin. Sin persuaded us to do something other than the righteousness in the Law, and therefore, demonstrated through the Law why we deserved death! Paul goes on to say that although he delights in God's Torah, his sinful nature is at war with it. He even asks the question, *"Who will rescue me…"* The conclusion is in:

Rom 8:1-4
8:1 Therefore, there is **now no condemnation** for those who are in Christ Jesus, 2 because through Christ Jesus the law of the Spirit of life set me free from the law of sin and death. 3 For what the law was powerless to do in that it was **weakened by the sinful nature**, God did by sending his own Son in the likeness of sinful man to be a sin offering. And so he condemned sin in sinful man, 4 in order that **the righteous requirements of the law might be fully met in us**, who do not live according to the sinful nature but according to the Spirit.

I said in the very beginning of this paper that:{I hope to persuade you not to throw out the "baby" (**Law**) with the "bath water" (**curse of the Law**). In Christ there is no longer any condemnation caused by man's weakness and inability to keep the Law. Through Jesus' work in removing the penalty of the Law the believer is set free from the demand for our death as a result of sin (*law of sin and death*) and is empowered to keep the righteous requirements of the Law(*law of the Spirit of life*) in our new life in Christ.} I believe that the reason I missed the correct interpretation of these passages for so many years was that I viewed the Law as bad. Truthfully, I was even surprised to see all of the positive adjectives referring to the Law in the Older and Newer Scriptures. This was an imbalance that needed to be corrected. Hopefully, after reading the 22,090 words that I have typed so far, you are at least open to the *"wonderful things"* in the Law and don't view the Law as contrary to faith. The Law points both to man's sin and God's righteousness. We are no longer subject to any condemnation caused by our weakness; we are free to do the good that the Law requires. The last scripture we will look at in Romans is:

Rom 10:4
4 Christ is the <u>end of the law</u> so that there may be righteousness for everyone who believes.

I am embarrassed that I held fervently to this scripture as definitive proof that the Mosaic Law no longer had any merit in our lives because it seems so basic now. Isn't revelation always that way? Once something becomes clear it is hard to imagine that you couldn't see it. I considered listing all the scripture that would be thoroughly invalidated if this rendering is accepted; but, I am fearful that would horribly belabor the points already made in Deuteronomy, Jeremiah, Ezekiel, Psalms, Acts, Romans, 2 Timothy, 1 John 5, and most of all *Matthew 5:17-19*:

17 "**Do not think that I have come to abolish** the Law or the Prophets; I have not come to abolish them but to fulfill them. 18 I tell you the truth, **until heaven and earth disappear, not the smallest letter, not the least stroke of a pen, will by any means disappear from the Law** until everything is accomplished. 19 Anyone who breaks one of the least of these commandments and teaches others to do the same will be called least in the kingdom of

heaven, but **whoever practices and teaches these commands will be called great in the kingdom of heaven**.

Jesus did not terminate the Law? He was the goal of the Law! I won't bore you with long excerpts from Lexicons, but the Greek word "telos" used in *Romans 10:4* as "*end*" can also mean "the goal of". It is translated that way in both of following passages:

1 Tim 1:5
5 The **goal** of this command is love, which comes from a pure heart and a good conscience and a sincere faith.

1 Peter 1:9
9 for you are receiving the **goal** of your faith, the salvation of your souls.

Why then is it translated as "*end*" in Romans? I believe it is because all translations involve interpretation to some degree and our translations have been given to us by people that don't have a foundation in the Torah that is comparable to the author of the passage…namely Paul. This is certainly not the only time a word's translation has been affected by the translator's cultural bias. Consider these two passages as an illustration:

James 2:1-2
My brothers, as believers in our glorious Lord Jesus Christ, don't show favoritism. 2 Suppose a man comes into your **meeting** wearing a gold ring and fine clothes, and a poor man in shabby clothes also comes in…

The Greek word "sunagoge" is translated as "*meeting*" in the book of James even though it is usually translated as synagogue. Could that be because the translators assumed that the meeting James was speaking of couldn't have been in a synagogue? Why, Paul taught in synagogues. Incidentally, the same translators had no problem identifying "sunagoge" as synagogue in **Revelation 2:9**, "*I know thy works, and tribulation, and poverty, (but thou art rich) and I know the blasphemy of them which say they are Jews, and are not, but are the **synagogue** of Satan.*" In other words, if "sunagoge" is used in a positive sense then it is an assembly or a meeting, but if it is used in a negative since then it has to be a synagogue. Don't get me wrong! I love the NIV and I don't have the credentials to critique it from a truly academic point of view, but all of our English translations lack the Jewish flavor that the scripture was written with. That is one reason that David Stern's Complete Jewish Bible has become so popular. Look how he translates the passage from Romans.

Romans 10:4-5 (The Complete Jewish Bible "formatting unaltered")
```
4For the goal at which the Torah
aims is the Messiah, who offers
righteousness to everyone who
trusts.  5For Moshe writes about
the righteousness grounded in the
Torah that the person who does
these things will attain life
through them.
```

What a dramatic difference that makes in ease of understanding. The Law aimed at teaching us to trust in the Messiah. If you simply must cling to the NIV translation of **Romans 10:4**, then you need to think of Jesus as the end of the journey that the Law put you on towards righteousness. In any case, I believe that "Spirit-Enriched" study will lead you to the conclusion that Jesus did not abolish the Law; just as He said that He wouldn't.

I am in a bit of a quandary, in that, no matter how many of the "problem" scriptures I cover, someone will say I avoided one because it destroys my interpretation. **My hearts desire is to promote a balanced view of the Law that acknowledges both its benefits and its limitations.** I have acknowledged frequently that some of these things are, as Peter said, "...*hard to understand*" In this attempt, I have to draw and end at some point or this paper turns into a commentary which was not my goal. The book of Hebrews causes many people difficulty; and yet, it is probably the most "Jewish" book in the Newer Testament. I don't want to cover Hebrews in the scope of this paper because I believe that with a few suggestions and a little guidance from the Holy Spirit the difficulties within the book will dissolve themselves. Here are a few observations:

- A large percentage of the Jewish people missed the intent of the Law. The norm for Judaism of Jesus' day was encrusted with legalism as a means of righteousness; but the purpose of the Law was to teach a righteous way to live while trusting in God for salvation.
- The Law prescribed sacrifices and a priesthood as a teaching tool for training in righteousness, but the realities are better and are found in Christ.
- The Melchizedek priesthood pre-dated the Aaronic priesthood and was foretold in the Torah as well as the Tanakh. (The Essene Community had a particular interest in the Melchizedek priesthood because they say the priesthood in their day as corrupt).
- Comparisons between priesthoods don't destroy the Law; they show us the way

we are intended to relate to the Law (this concept maybe referred to as change; as in, a change in the way we relate to the Law not abolish it). For instance, our relationship to the sacrificial system is to understand that it was a "*shadow*" of things to come. It is the sacrificial system which was vanishing and soon to pass away (with the destruction of the temple).
- I believe the emphasis of the book is on Jewish believers (maybe Essenes) who were being tempted in the face of severe trial (possibly the Jewish rebellion that was being crushed) to revert to or trust in ritual purity for salvation and deliverance.
- The essence of the Torah is not ritualistic sacrifice; God was after hearts like David. The lack of a temple does not destroy the Law.

The last "problem" scriptures that I will address in this paper before closing are in the Corinthian letters.

The Corinthian Epistles

For the sake of flow, let me start with:

2 Cor 3:5-11
6 He has made us competent as ministers of a new covenant- — not of the letter but of the Spirit; for the letter kills, but the Spirit gives life.

I have already made the point several times that the Torah pronounces penalties demanding punishment (even death) for sin. The primary difference in the Newer Covenant is the way we relate to the Law. Although the Law was intended to bring life, it actually brought death (***Romans 7:10***) This is not because the Law was bad or sinful! (***Romans 7:7***) Instead the Law is holy, righteous, good, and spiritual (**Romans 7:12 & 14**) but we were unspiritual, proved unrighteous, not having goodness. The promise of Jeremiah & Ezekiel, eluded to in the analogy in **2 Corinthians 3:3**, was that the Law that had been written in stone and on scrolls would be impressed on the human heart and mind. Furthermore, God's own Spirit would move you to understand and keep the Law. ***2 Corinthians 3:3*** is an affirmation of the internalization of the Law not the abolishment of it. The primary advantage in the Newer Covenant is that the penalties demanding death have been removed and the Holy Spirit empowers us to keep the Law; showing us an abundant full life that is free from condemnation. ***Romans 8:1-11*** teaches this very concept!

7 Now if the ministry that brought death, which was engraved in letters on stone, came with glory, so that the Israelites could not look steadily at the face of Moses because of its glory, fading though it was, 8 will not the ministry of the Spirit be even more glorious? 9 If the ministry that condemns men is glorious, how much more glorious is the ministry that brings righteousness! 10 For what was glorious has no glory now **in comparison** with the surpassing glory.

The norm in Judaism of Jesus' day tended towards legalistic observance of the Law in a vain hope for salvation. This concept is continually being "hammered" by Paul because that was never the purpose of the Torah. What a shock it must have been to some Jews to hear Paul talking about the Torah as a "*ministry of death*" as opposed to "*giving light to the eyes*" (***Psalm 19:8***). Isn't that precisely why God used Paul to say these things as opposed to someone else? Paul was a Pharisee and his love and loyalty to the Torah was never in question. He was uniquely able to point out the short comings of the Mosaic Covenant without the audience misunderstanding him as being anti-Torah. The phrase *"ministry of death"* refers to the fact that men are sinful and the Torah is holy. The penalty for sin is death according to the righteous standards of God. Paul is saying you believed the Torah was good (rightly so) and it condemns you; How much better is the new relationship by way of the Spirit that frees you from condemnation and empowers you to do what the Torah required.

11 And if what was fading away came with glory, how much greater is the glory of that which lasts!

In covering **Romans 10:4** and all of the preceding pages, I have explained the way in which the Law endures for ever. It is the *"curses of the Law"* supremely illustrated through the Temple sacrificial system which was fading away. They found their fulfillment in Christ and the Temple was about to be destroyed. The righteous standards or Law of God never fades away! Read these three quotations from the Tanakh: (I have not quoted these, previously, in this paper)

Isa 2:3-4
3 Many peoples will come and say, "Come, let us go up to the mountain of the LORD,
to the house of the God of Jacob. He will **teach us his ways, so that we may walk in his paths**." **The law will go out from Zion**, the word of the LORD from Jerusalem. 4 He will judge between the nations and will settle disputes for many peoples. They will beat their swords into plowshares and their spears into pruning hooks. Nation will not take up sword against nation, nor will they train for war anymore.

Isa 51:4-7
4 "Listen to me, my people; hear me, my nation:
The law will go out from me;
my justice will become a light to the nations. 5 My righteousness draws near speedily, my salvation is on the way, and my arm will bring justice to the nations. The islands will look to me and wait in hope for my arm. 6 Lift up your eyes to the heavens, look at the earth beneath; the heavens will vanish like smoke, the earth will wear out like a garment and its inhabitants die like flies. But my salvation will last forever, my righteousness will never fail. 7 "**Hear me, you who know what is right, you people who have my law in your hearts**:

Mic 4:2-3
2 Many nations will come and say,
"Come, let us go up to the mountain of the LORD,
to the house of the God of Jacob.
He will teach us his ways,
so that we may walk in his paths."
The law will go out from Zion,
the word of the LORD from Jerusalem.
3 He will judge between many peoples
and will settle disputes for strong nations far and wide.

You can see that even in the Millennial Reign the Law is present. Isaiah, Micah, and their audiences all had the Torah in mind in these references. In fact, one way that the Law lasts forever is in its truest representation, Jesus! He kept it perfectly and we are credited with that perfection in Him. Now we must (by the Spirit) walk as He walked. Let's finish the passage in 2 Corinthians.

2 Cor 3:12-18
12 Therefore, since we have such a hope, we are very bold. 13 We are not like Moses, who would put a veil over his face to keep the Israelites from gazing at it while the radiance was fading away. 14 But their minds were made dull, for to this day **the same veil remains when the old covenant is read**. It has not been removed, because **only in Christ is it taken away**. 15 Even to this day when Moses is read, **a veil covers their hearts**. 16 But whenever anyone turns to the Lord, the veil is taken away. 17 Now the Lord is the Spirit, and where the Spirit of the Lord is, there is freedom.

Paul is using a metaphor regarding the *"veil"*. His point is that in Christ we see the true intent of the Law, but those outside of Christ can't see it until the veil is taken away. The Lord's Spirit is the key to seeing the freedom that comes from the Law. Ironically, I was somewhat veiled to the "wonderful things" in the Law and I couldn't see freedom. In Christ, that veil is removed! I am free from condemnation and free to do the good that the Law requires. As James says, *"the man who looks intently into the perfect law that gives freedom, and continues to do this, not forgetting what he has heard, but doing it — he will be blessed in what he does.* Read one last Psalm passage and then we will close.

Ps 119:44-48
44 I will always obey your law, for ever and ever. 45 I will walk about in freedom, for I have sought out your precepts. 46 I will speak of your statutes before kings and will not be put to shame, 47 for I delight in your commands because I love them. 48 I lift up my hands to your commands, which I love, and I meditate on your decrees.

As Christians, we are free! We are not under any system of cursing for our failings. This allows us to truly be free in attempting to do good at all times to all men with out fear of failure of or judgment. This freedom should be used wisely to make the Gospel understandable and appealing to all that Jesus would call.

1 Cor 9:19-22
19 Though I am free and belong to no man, I make myself a slave to everyone, to win as many as possible. 20 To the Jews I became like a Jew, to win the Jews. To those under the law I became like one under the law (though I myself am not under the law), so as to win those under the law. 21 To those not having the law I became like one not having the law (though I am not free from God's law but am under Christ's law), so as to win those not having the law. 22 To the weak I became weak, to win the weak. I have become all things to all men so that by all possible means I might save some.

Paul was not *"under the law"*; in that, he was not subject to its penalties, but he never saw himself as *"free from God's law"*. He related to God's Law in and through Christ. I am not trying to compel anyone to place themselves under the penalty of the Law. I am advocating the freedom for any believer (Jew or Gentile) to engage in the *"wonderful things"* found in the Law without fear of being labeled as *"under the Law"*. The legalistic "Judaizing" environment, in which, the Church was born is no longer the prevailing force. Paul and the other Jewish Apostles triumphed in allowing the Gentile believers to rush into the Church free of burden. Now "the shoe is on the other foot"! The Church has been thoroughly Hellenized, and has completely lost all identifying marks of its Jewish heritage. I am concerned that this Hellenization has stripped the Gospel of the very culture that birthed it, and worse of all, has made it unpalatable for the natural descendants of Jacob. We have been so skewed that we refused to even recognize the Mosaic Law as teaching us beneficial things for daily living. Unfortunately, I could envision a scenario were the present day Church would rebuff a nationalistic Jew (like a young Saul of Tarsus) with the words, "Law don't go round here, Law Dawg"! While my envisioned scenario is obviously embellished, it is certainly what we do in principle when we show absolutely no regard for the Law or the culture that it sponsored. A balanced, biblical view of the Law is important for the growth of even Gentile believers, but it is indispensable to the effort to win some of Paul's own people. It is true that the Law and the Prophets can be abridged and condensed to say *"Love the Lord your God with all of your heart, with all of your mind, and with all of your strength"* but wouldn't it be good to know how that conclusion was drawn?

Deut 6:4-7
4 Hear, O Israel: The LORD our God, the LORD is one. 5 Love the LORD your God with all your heart and with all your soul and with all your strength. 6 **These commandments that I give you today are to be upon your hearts. 7 Impress them on your children. Talk about them when you sit at home and when you walk along the road, when you lie down and when you get up.**

Perhaps, it is time we put the command above into practice. I am convinced that the study of the Law will not hinder your walk, it will deepen it. Micah came to the following conclusion after living "in the Law" his whole life:

Mic 6:8
8 He has showed you, O man, what is good. And what does the LORD require of you? To act justly and to love mercy and to walk humbly with your God.

I pray that this work has added something to your walk with God and has helped to bring into focus the righteous intent of the Law. My email address is estephens@onelifechanged.com and my Church website it www.onelifechanged.com or www.1lifechanged.com if you would like to correspond.

Enthralled with Him,

Eric Stephens
Life Changing Ministries

Post Statement: I have not knowingly quoted any books or authors without mentioning it in the body of this document. When quoting the Bible I use the NIV translation unless I noted otherwise. Below I am going to list a few books that have been useful in my studies but I must include a word of caution: The authors of these books are scholarly but that doesn't make them the final authority. In each of these books, I found concepts that (in my view) are to be disregarded. With that word of warning, when considering a man's life work or his theology, we need the maturity to avoid being overly critical of minor areas of difference. Furthermore, it is unfair to read only portions of an author's book and then assume the rest. These books cover complicated subject matter and deserve to be read in their entirety. Avoid making the shameful mistake of, "throwing away" a person's contribution to the Kingdom simply because they are different than you. The list of books is as follows:

Our Father Abraham by Marvin R. Wilson, Ph.D.

They Love the Torah by David Friedman, Ph.D.

Restoring the Jewishness of the Gospel by David H. Stern

***Yeshua* A Guide to the Real Jesus and the Original Church** by Dr. Ron Moseley

Jewish Roots by Dan Juster

I started writing this paper on Saturday, October 15th, 2005. I had ordered a commentary that didn't come in until two days before I finished writing this document (I finished Oct. 21st). Upon examining the commentary, I was at a lose as to how I should feel. The commentary clarified nearly everything I was attempting to address and did so in a scholarly fashion that is beyond me. I encourage you to get it and read it. The commentary is:

The Jewish New Testament Commentary by David H. Stern

I have also had the Complete Jewish Bible that he wrote for a couple of years and have been thoroughly blessed by it.

www.ingramcontent.com/pod-product-compliance
Lightning Source LLC
Chambersburg PA
CBHW032004060426
42449CB00031B/496